AN INTRUDER

Martin Rattler

OR

A Boy's Adventures in the Forests of Brazil

By

Robert Michael Ballantyne

Author of "The Dog Crusoe and his Master," "The Young Fur-Traders,"
"The Gorilla Hunters," "Ungava,"
"The Coral Island,"
&c.

NEW EDITION

T. NELSON AND SONS
LONDON · EDINBURGH
NEW YORK

1893

PREFACE.

My dear young Readers, in presenting this book to you I have only to repeat what I have said in the prefaces of my former works—namely, that all the important points and anecdotes are true; only the minor and unimportant ones being mingled with fiction. With this single remark, I commit my work to your hands, and wish you a pleasant ramble, in spirit, through the romantic forests of Brazil.

Yours affectionately,

R. M. BALLANTYNE.

CONTENTS.

CHAPTER I.
The hero and his only relative..9

CHAPTER II.
In disgrace...14

CHAPTER III.
The great fight..18

CHAPTER IV.
A lesson to all stocking-knitters—Martin's prospects begin to open up......30

CHAPTER V.
Martin, being willing to go to sea, goes to sea against his will.................37

CHAPTER VI.
The voyage—A pirate, chase, wreck, and escape..............................47

CHAPTER VII.
Martin and Barney get lost in a great forest, where they see strange and terrible things...54

CHAPTER VIII.
An enchanting land—An uncomfortable bed, and a queer breakfast—Many surprises and a few frights, together with a notable discovery............62

CHAPTER IX.
The hermit...75

CONTENTS.

CHAPTER X.
An enemy in the night—The vampire bat—The hermit discourses on strange, and curious, and interesting things..................81

CHAPTER XI.
The hermit's story..................90

CHAPTER XII.
A hunting expedition, in which are seen stones that can run, and cows that require no food—Besides a desperate encounter with a jaguar, and other strange things..................106

CHAPTER XIII.
Martin and Barney continue their travels, and see strange things—Among others, they see living jewels—They go to see a festa—They fight and run away..................123

CHAPTER XIV.
Cogitations and canoeing on the Amazon—Barney's exploit with an alligator—Stubborn facts—Remarkable mode of sleeping..................137

CHAPTER XV.
The great anaconda's dinner—Barney gets a fright—Turtles' eggs—A satisfactory "blow out"—Senhor Antonio's plantation—Preparations for a great hunt..................150

CHAPTER XVI.
An alligator hunt—Remarkable explosions—The rainy season ushered in by an awful resurrection..................162

CHAPTER XVII.
The Gapo—Interruptions—Grampus and Marmoset—Canoeing in the woods—A night on a floating island..................176

CHAPTER XVIII.
The sad and momentous era referred to at the close of the chapter preceding the last..................186

CHAPTER XIX.
Worse and worse—Everything seems to go wrong together..................195

CONTENTS.

CHAPTER XX.
Martin reflects much, and forms a firm resolve—The Indian village 204

CHAPTER XXI.
Savage feasts and ornaments—Martin grows desperate, and makes a bold attempt to escape..213

CHAPTER XXII.
The escape—Alone in the wilderness—Fight between a jaguar and an alligator—Martin encounters strange and terrible creatures................224

CHAPTER XXIII.
Martin meets with friends, and visits the diamond mines 236

CHAPTER XXIV.
The diamond mines—More and more astonishing!..............................242

CHAPTER XXV.
New scenes and pleasant travelling..265

CHAPTER XXVI.
The return...276

CHAPTER XXVII.
The old garret..283

CHAPTER XXVIII.
Conclusion..289

MARTIN RATTLER.

CHAPTER I.

The hero and his only relative.

MARTIN RATTLER was a very bad boy. At least his aunt, Mrs. Dorothy Grumbit, said so; and certainly she ought to have known, if anybody should, for Martin lived with her, and was, as she herself expressed it, "the bane of her existence, the very torment of her life." No doubt of it whatever, according to Aunt Dorothy Grumbit's showing, Martin Rattler was "a remarkably bad boy."

It is a curious fact, however, that although most of the people in the village of Ashford seemed to agree with Mrs. Grumbit in her opinion of Martin, there were very few of them who did not smile cheerfully on the child when they met him, and say, "Good-day, lad," as heartily as if they thought him the best boy in the place. No one seemed to bear

Martin Rattler ill-will, notwithstanding his alleged badness. Men laughed when they said he was a bad boy, as if they did not quite believe their own assertion. The vicar, an old white-headed man, with a kind, hearty countenance, said that the child was full of mischief—full of mischief; but he would improve as he grew older, he was quite certain of that. And the vicar was a good judge, for he had five boys of his own, besides three other boys, the sons of a distant relative, who boarded with him; and he had lived forty years in a parish overflowing with boys, and he was particularly fond of boys in general. Not so the doctor, a pursy little man with a terrific frown, who hated boys, especially little ones, with a very powerful hatred. The doctor said that Martin was a scamp.

And yet Martin had not the appearance of a scamp. He had fat rosy cheeks, a round rosy mouth, a straight, delicately-formed nose, a firm, massive chin, and a broad forehead. But the latter was seldom visible, owing to the thickly-clustering fair curls that overhung it. When asleep, Martin's face was the perfection of gentle innocence. But the instant he opened his dark-brown eyes, a thousand dimples and wrinkles played over his visage, chiefly at the corners of his mouth and round his eyes, as if the spirit of fun and the spirit of mischief had got entire possession of the boy, and were determined to make the most of him. When deeply interested in anything, Martin was as grave and serious as a philosopher.

Aunt Dorothy Grumbit had a turned-up nose— a very much turned-up nose; so much so, indeed, that it presented a front view of the nostrils! It was an aggravating nose, too, for the old lady's spectacles refused to rest on any part of it except the extreme point. Mrs. Grumbit invariably placed them on the right part of her nose, and they as invariably slid down the curved slope until they were brought up by the little hillock at the end. There they condescended to repose in peace.

Mrs. Grumbit was mild, and gentle, and little, and thin, and old—perhaps seventy-five; but no one knew her age for certain, not even herself. She wore an old-fashioned, high-crowned cap, and a gown of bed-curtain chintz, with flowers on it the size of a saucer. It was a curious gown, and very cheap, for Mrs. Grumbit was poor. No one knew the extent of her poverty any more than they did her age; but she herself knew it, and felt it deeply— never so deeply, perhaps, as when her orphan nephew Martin grew old enough to be put to school and she had not wherewithal to send him. But love is quick-witted and resolute. A residence of six years in Germany had taught her to knit stockings at a rate that cannot be described, neither conceived unless seen. She knitted two dozen pairs. The vicar took one dozen, the doctor took the other. The fact soon became known. Shops were not numerous in the village in those days, and the wares they supplied were only second-rate. Orders came pouring in; Mrs. Grumbit's knitting-wires clicked, and her little old hands wagged with incomprehensible rapidity and unflagging regularity; and Martin Rattler was sent to school.

While occupied with her knitting she sat in a high-backed chair in a very small deep window, through which the sun streamed nearly the whole day, and out of which there was the most charming imaginable view of the gardens and orchards of the villagers, with a little dancing brook in the midst, and the green fields of the farmers beyond, studded with sheep and cattle and knolls of woodland, and bounded in the far distance by the bright blue sea. It was a lovely scene, such an one as causes the eye to brighten and the heart to melt as we gaze upon it and think, perchance, of its Creator.

Yes, it was a scene worth looking at; but Mrs. Grumbit never looked at it, for the simple reason that she could not have seen it if she had. Half way across her own little parlour was the extent of her natural vision. By the aid of spectacles and a steady, concentrated effort she could see the fireplace at the other end of the room, and the portrait of her deceased husband, who had been a sea-captain, and the white kitten that usually sat on the rug before the fire. To be sure she saw them very indistinctly. The picture was a hazy blue patch, which was the captain's coat; with a white patch down the middle of it, which was his waistcoat; and a yellow ball on the top of it, which was his head. It was rather an indistinct and generalized view, no doubt, but she *saw* it, and that was a great comfort.

CHAPTER II.

In disgrace.

FIRE was the cause of Martin's getting into disgrace at school for the first time; and this is how it happened.

"Go and poke the fire, Martin Rattler," said the schoolmaster, "and put on a bit of coal; and see that you don't send the sparks flying about the floor."

Martin sprang with alacrity to obey, for he was standing up with the class at the time, and was glad of the temporary relaxation. He stirred the fire with great care, and put on several pieces of coal very slowly, and rearranged them two or three times; after which he stirred the fire a little more, and examined it carefully to see that it was all right. But he did not seem quite satisfied, and was proceeding to readjust the coals when Bob Croaker, one of the big boys, who was a bullying, ill-tempered fellow, and had a spite against Martin, called out,—

"Please, sir, Rattler's playin' at the fire."

"Come back to your place, sir!" cried the master sternly.

Martin returned in haste, and resumed his position in the class. As he did so he observed that his forefinger was covered with soot. Immediately a smile of glee overspread his features, and while the master was busy with one of the boys, he drew his black finger gently down the forehead and nose of the boy next to him.

"What part of the earth was peopled by the descendants of Ham?" cried the master, pointing to the dux.

"Shem," shrieked a small boy near the foot of the class.

"Silence!" thundered the master, with a frown that caused the small boy to quake down to the points of his toes.

"Asia," answered dux.

"Next?"

"Turkey."

"Next, next, next? Hallo! John Ward," cried the master, starting up in anger from his seat, "what do you mean by that, sir?"

"What, sir?" said John Ward, tremulously, while a suppressed titter ran round the class.

"Your face, sir! Who blacked your face, eh?"

"I—I—don't know," said the boy, drawing his sleeve across his face, which had the effect of covering it with sooty streaks.

An uncontrollable shout of laughter burst from the whole school, which was instantly followed by a silence so awful and profound that a pin might have been heard to fall.

"Martin Rattler, you did that! I know you did; I see the marks on your fingers. Come here, sir! Now tell me, *did* you do it?"

Martin Rattler never told falsehoods. His old aunt had laboured to impress upon him from infancy that to lie was to commit a sin which is abhorred by God and scorned by man, and her teaching had not been in vain. The child would have suffered any punishment rather than have told a deliberate lie. He looked straight in the master's face, and said, "Yes, sir, I did it."

"Very well, go to your seat, and remain in school during the play-hour."

With a heavy heart Martin obeyed, and soon after the school was dismissed.

"I say, Rattler," whispered Bob Croaker, as he passed, "I'm going to teach your white kitten to swim just now. Won't you come and see it?"

The malicious laugh with which the boy accompanied this remark convinced Martin that he intended to put his threat in execution. For a moment he thought of rushing out after him to protect his pet kitten; but a glance at the stern brow of the master, as he sat at his desk reading, restrained him, so, crushing down his feelings of mingled fear and anger, he endeavoured to while away the time by watching the boys as they played in the fields before the windows of the school.

CHAPTER III.

The great fight.

"MARTIN!" said the schoolmaster, in a severe tone, looking up from the book with which he was engaged, "don't look out at the window, sir; turn your back to it."

"Please, sir, I can't help it," replied the boy, trembling with eagerness as he stared across the fields.

"Turn your back on it, I say!" reiterated the master in a loud tone, at the same time striking the desk violently with his cane.

"O sir, let me out! There's Bob Croaker with my kitten. He's going to drown it. I know he is—he said he would; and if he does, aunty will die, for she loves it next to me. And I *must* save it; and—and if you *don't* let me out—you'll be a murderer!"

At this concluding burst, Martin sprang forward and stood before his master with clinched fists and a face blazing with excitement. The schoolmaster's gaze of astonishment gradually gave place to a dark frown strangely mingled with a smile, and, when the boy concluded, he said quietly, "You may go."

No second bidding was needed. The door flew open with a bang, and the gravel of the playground, spurned right and left, dashed against the window panes as Martin flew across it. The paling that fenced it off from the fields below was low, but too high for a jump. Never a boy in all the school had crossed that paling at a spring without laying his hands upon it, but Martin did. We do not mean to say that he did anything superhuman; but he rushed at it like a charge of cavalry, sprang from the ground like a deer, kicked away the top bar, tumbled completely over, landed on his head, and rolled down the slope on the other side as fast as he could have run down—perhaps faster.

It would have required sharper eyes than yours or mine to have observed how Martin got on his legs again; but he did it in a twinkling, and was half across the field almost before you could wink, and panting on the heels of Bob Croaker. Bob saw him coming, and instantly started off at a hard run, followed by the whole school. A few minutes brought them to the banks of the stream, where Bob Croaker halted, and, turning round, held the white kitten up by the nape of the neck.

"Oh, spare it! spare it, Bob!—don't do it—please don't, don't do it!" gasped Martin, as he strove in vain to run faster.

"There you go!" shouted Bob, with a coarse laugh, sending the kitten high into the air, whence it fell with a loud splash into the water.

It was a dreadful shock to feline nerves, no doubt, but that white kitten was no ordinary animal. Its little heart beat bravely when it rose to the surface, and before its young master came up it had regained the bank. But, alas! what a change! It went into the stream a fat, round, comfortable ball of eiderdown; it came out—a scraggy blotch of white paint, with its black eyes glaring like two great glass beads! No sooner did it crawl out of the water than Bob Croaker seized it, and whirled it round his head, amid suppressed cries of "Shame!" intending to throw it in again; but at that instant Martin Rattler seized Bob by the collar of his coat with both hands, and letting himself drop suddenly, dragged the cruel boy to the ground, while the kitten crept humbly away and hid itself in a thick tuft of grass.

A moment sufficed to enable Bob Croaker, who was nearly twice Martin's weight, to free himself from the grasp of his panting antagonist, whom he threw on his back, and doubled his fist, intending to strike Martin on the face; but a general rush of the boys prevented this.

"Shame, shame! fair play!" cried several; "don't hit him when he's down!"

"Then let him rise up and come on!" cried Bob fiercely, as he sprang up and released Martin.

"Ay, that's fair. Now then, Martin, remember the kitten."

"Strike men of your own size!" cried several of the bigger boys, as they interposed to prevent Martin from rushing into the unequal contest.

"So I will," cried Bob Croaker, glaring round with passion. "Come on, any of you that likes. I don't care a button for the biggest of you."

No one accepted this challenge, for Bob was the oldest and the strongest boy in the school, although, as is usually the case with bullies, by no means the bravest.

Seeing that no one intended to fight with him, and that a crowd of boys strove to hold Martin Rattler back, while they assured him that he had not the smallest chance in the world, Bob turned towards the kitten, which was quietly and busily employed in licking itself dry, and said, "Now, Martin, you coward, I'll give it another swim for your impudence."

"Stop, stop!" cried Martin earnestly. "Bob Croaker, I would rather do anything than fight. I would give you everything I have to save my kitten; but if you won't spare it unless I fight, I'll do it. If you throw it in before you fight me, you're the greatest coward that ever walked. Just give me five minutes to breathe, and a drink of water, and I'll fight you as long as I can stand."

Bob looked at his little foe in surprise. "Well, that's fair. I'm your man; but if you don't lick me, I'll drown the kitten, that's all." Having said this, he quietly divested himself of his jacket and neckcloth, while several boys assisted Martin to do the same, and brought him a draught of water in the crown of one of their caps. In five minutes all was ready, and the two boys stood face to face and foot to foot, with their fists doubled, and revolving, and a ring of boys around them.

Just at this critical moment the kitten, having found the process of licking itself dry more fatiguing than it had expected, gave vent to a faint mew of distress. It was all that was wanting to set Martin's indignant heart into a blaze of inexpressible fury. Bob Croaker's visage instantly received a shower of sharp, stinging blows, that had the double effect of taking that youth by surprise and throwing him down upon the greensward. But Martin could not hope to do this a second time. Bob now knew the vigour of his assailant, and braced himself warily to the combat, commencing operations by giving Martin a tremendous blow on the point of his nose, and another on the chest. These had the effect of tempering Martin's rage with a salutary degree of caution, and of eliciting from the spectators sundry cries of warning on the one hand, and admiration on the other, while the young champions revolved warily round each other, and panted vehemently.

The battle that was fought that day was one of a thousand. It created as great a sensation in the village school as did the battle of Waterloo in England. It was a notable fight, such as had not taken place within the memory of the oldest boy in the village, and from which, in after years, events of juvenile history were dated — especially pugilistic events, of which, when a good one came off, it used to be said that "such a battle had not taken place since the year of the *Great Fight.*" Bob Croaker was a noted fighter. Martin Rattler was, up to this date, an untried hero. Although fond of rough play and boisterous mischief, he had an unconquerable aversion to *earnest* fighting, and very rarely indeed returned home with a black eye—much to the satisfaction of Aunt Dorothy Grumbit, who objected to all fighting from principle, and frequently asserted, in gentle tones, that there should be no soldiers or sailors (fighting sailors, she meant) at all, but that people ought all to settle everything the best way they could without fighting, and live peaceably with one another, as the Bible told them to do. They would be far happier and better off, she was sure of that; and if everybody was of her way of thinking, there would be neither swords, nor guns, nor pistols, nor squibs, nor anything else at all! Dear old lady! It would indeed be a blessing if her principles could be carried out in this warring and jarring world. But as this is rather difficult, what we ought to be careful about is, that we never fight except in a good cause and with a clear conscience.

It was well for Martin Rattler, on that great day, that the formation of the ground favoured him. The spot on which the fight took place was uneven, and covered with little hillocks and hollows, over which Bob Croaker stumbled and into which he fell—being a clumsy boy on his legs—and did himself considerable damage; while Martin, who was firmly knit and active as a kitten, scarcely ever fell, or, if he did, sprang up again like an indiarubber ball. Fair play was embedded deep in the centre of Martin's heart, so that he scorned to hit his adversary when he was down or in the act of rising; but the thought of the fate that awaited the white kitten if he were conquered acted like lightning in his veins, and scarcely had Bob time to double his fists after a fall, when he was knocked back again into the hollow out of which he had risen. There were no *rounds* in this fight— no pausing to recover breath. Martin's anger rose with every blow, whether given or received; and although he was knocked down flat four or five times, he rose again, and, without a second's delay, rushed headlong at his enemy. Feeling that he was too little and light to make much impression on Bob Croaker by means of mere blows, he endeavoured as much as possible to throw his weight against him at each assault; but Bob stood his ground well, and after a time seemed even to be recovering strength a little.

Suddenly he made a rush at Martin, and, dealing him a successful blow on the forehead, knocked him down; at the same time he himself tripped over a mole-hill and fell upon his face. Both were on their legs in an instant. Martin grew desperate. The white kitten swimming for its life seemed to rise before him, and new energy was infused into his frame. He retreated a step or two, and then darted forward like an arrow from a bow. Uttering a loud cry, he sprang completely in the air and plunged—head and fists together, as if he were taking a dive—into Bob Croaker's bosom! The effect was tremendous. Bob went down like a shock of grain before the sickle; and having, in their prolonged movements, approached close to the brink of the stream, both he and Martin went with a sounding splash into the deep pool and disappeared. It was but for a moment, however. Martin's head emerged first, with eyes and mouth distended to the utmost. Instantly, on finding bottom, he turned to deal his opponent another blow; but it was not needed. When Bob Croaker's head rose to the surface there was no motion in the features, and the eyes were closed. The intended blow was changed into a friendly grasp, and exerting himself to the utmost, Martin dragged his insensible schoolfellow to the bank, where, in a few minutes, he recovered sufficiently to declare in a sulky tone that he would fight no more.

"Bob Croaker," said Martin, holding out his hand, "I'm sorry we've had to fight. I wouldn't have done it but to save my kitten. You compelled me to do it, you know that. Come, let's be friends again."

Bob made no reply, but slowly and with some difficulty put on his vest and jacket.

"I'm sure," continued Martin, "there's no reason in bearing me ill-will. I've done nothing unfair, and I'm very sorry we've had to fight. Won't you shake hands?"

Bob was silent.

"Come, come, Bob!" cried several of the bigger boys, "don't be sulky, man; shake hands and be friends. Martin has licked you this time, and you'll lick him next time, no doubt, and that's all about it."

"Arrah, then, ye're out there intirely. Bob Croaker'll niver lick Martin Rattler, though he wos to live to the age of the great M'Thuselah," said a deep-toned voice close to the spot where the fight had taken place.

All eyes were instantly turned in the direction whence it proceeded, and the boys now became aware, for the first time, that the combat had been witnessed by a sailor, who, with a smile of approval beaming on his good-humoured countenance, sat under the shade of a neighbouring tree smoking a pipe of that excessive shortness and blackness that seems to be peculiarly beloved by Irishmen in the humbler ranks of life. The man was very tall and broad-shouldered, and carried himself with a free-and-easy swagger, as he rose and approached the group of boys.

"He'll niver bate ye, Martin, avic, as long as there's two timbers of ye houldin' togither." The seaman patted Martin on the head as he spoke; and, turning to Bob Croaker, continued: "Ye ought to be proud, ye spalpeen, o' bein' wopped by sich a young hero as this. Come here and shake hands with him; d'ye hear? Troth, an' it's besmearin' ye with too much honour that same. There, that'll do. Don't say ye're sorry now, for it's lies ye'd be tellin' if ye did. Come along, Martin, an' I'll convarse with ye as ye go home. Ye'll be a man yet, as sure as my name is Barney O'Flannagan."

Martin took the white kitten in his arms and thrust its wet little body into his equally wet bosom, where the warmth began soon to exercise a soothing influence on the kitten's depressed spirits, so that, ere long, it began to purr. He then walked with the sailor towards the village, with his face black and blue, and swelled and covered with blood, while Bob Croaker and his companions returned to the school.

The distance to Martin's residence was not great, but it was sufficient to enable the voluble Irishman to recount a series of the most wonderful adventures and stories of foreign lands that set Martin's heart on fire with desire to go to sea—a desire which was by no means new to him, and which recurred violently every time he paid a visit to the small sea-port of Bilton, which lay about five miles to the southward of his native village. Moreover, Barney suggested that it was time Martin should be doing for himself (he was now ten years old), and said that if he would join his ship he could get him a berth, for he was much in want of an active lad to help him with the coppers. But Martin Rattler sighed deeply, and said that, although his heart was set upon going to sea, he did not see how it was to be managed, for his aunt would not let him go.

Before they separated, however, it was arranged that Martin should pay the sailor's ship a visit, when he would hear a good deal more about foreign lands; and that, in the meantime, he should make another attempt to induce Aunt Dorothy Grumbit to give her consent to his going to sea.

CHAPTER IV.

A lesson to all stocking-knitters—Martin's prospects begin to open up.

IN the small sea-port of Bilton, before mentioned, there dwelt an old and wealthy merchant and ship-owner, who devoted a small portion of his time to business, and a very large portion of it to what is usually termed " doing good." This old gentleman was short, and stout, and rosy, and bald, and active, and sharp as a needle.

In the short time that Mr. Arthur Jollyboy devoted to business, he accomplished as much as most men do in the course of a long day. There was not a benevolent society in the town of which Arthur Jollyboy, Esquire, of the Old Hulk (as he styled his cottage), was not a member, director, secretary, and treasurer, all in one, and all at once! If it had been possible for man to be ubiquitous, Mr. Jollyboy would have been so naturally, or, if not naturally, he would have made himself so by force of will. Yet he made no talk about it. His step was quiet, though quick;

and his voice was gentle, though rapid; and he was chiefly famous for *talking* little and *doing* much.

Some time after the opening of our tale, Mr. Jollyboy had received information of Mrs. Grumbit's stocking movement. That same afternoon he put on his broad-brimmed white hat, and walking out to the village in which she lived, called upon the vicar, who was a particular and intimate friend of his. Having ascertained from the vicar that Mrs. Grumbit would not accept of charity, he said abruptly,—

" And why not—is she too proud ? "

" By no means," replied the vicar. " She says that she would think shame to take money from friends as long as she can work, because every penny that she would thus get would be so much less to go to the helpless poor, of whom, she says, with much truth, there are enough and to spare. And I quite agree with her as regards her principle; but it does not apply fully to her, for she cannot work so as to procure a sufficient livelihood without injury to her health."

" Is she clever ? " inquired Mr. Jollyboy.

" Why, no, not particularly. In fact, she does not often exert her reasoning faculties, except in the commonplace matters of ordinary and everyday routine."

"Then she's cleverer than most people," said Mr. Jollyboy, shortly. "Is she obstinate?"

"No, not in the least," returned the vicar with a puzzled smile.

"Ah, well, good-bye, good-bye; that's all I want to know."

Mr. Jollyboy rose, and hurrying through the village tapped at the cottage door, and was soon closeted with Mrs. Dorothy Grumbit. In the course of half-an-hour, Mr. Jollyboy drew from Mrs. Grumbit as much about her private affairs as he could, without appearing rude. But he found the old lady very close and sensitive on that point. Not so, however, when he got her upon the subject of her nephew. She had enough, and more than enough, to say about him. It is true she began by remarking sadly that he was a very bad boy; but as she continued to talk about him, she somehow or other gave her visitor the impression that he was a very *good* boy! They had a wonderfully long and confidential talk about Martin, during which Mr. Jollyboy struck Mrs. Grumbit nearly dumb with horror by stating positively that he would do for the boy—he would send him to sea! Then, seeing that he had hit the wrongest possible nail on the head, he said that he would make the lad a clerk in his office, where he would be sure to rise to a place of trust; whereat Mrs. Grumbit danced, if we may so speak, into herself for joy.

"And now, ma'am, about these stockings. I want two thousand pairs as soon as I can get them!"

"Sir?" said Mrs. Grumbit.

"Of course, not for my own use, ma'am; nor for the use of my family, for I have no family, and if I had, that would be an unnecessarily large supply. The fact is, Mrs. Grumbit, I am a merchant, and I send very large supplies of home-made articles to foreign lands, and two thousand pairs of socks are a mere driblet. Of course I do not expect you to make them all for me, but I wish you to make as many pairs as you can."

"I shall be very happy—" began Mrs. Grumbit.

"But, Mrs. Grumbit, there is a peculiar formation which I require in my socks that will give you extra trouble, I fear; but I must have it, whatever the additional expense may be. What is your charge for the pair you are now making?"

"Three shillings," said Mrs. Grumbit.

"Ah! very good. Now, take up the wires, if you please, ma'am, and do what I tell you. Now, drop that stitch—good; and take up this one—capital; and pull this one across that way—so; and that one across this way—exactly. Now, what is the result?"

The result was a complicated knot; and Mrs. Grumbit, after staring a few seconds at the old gentleman in surprise, said so, and begged to know what use it was of.

"Oh, never mind, never mind. We merchants have strange fancies, and foreigners have curious tastes now and then. Please to make all my socks with a hitch like that in them all round, just above the ankle. It will form an ornamental ring. I'm sorry to put you to the trouble, but of course I pay extra for fancy-work. Will six shillings a pair do for these?"

"My dear sir," said Mrs. Grumbit, "it is no additional—"

"Well, well, never mind," said Mr. Jollyboy. "Two thousand pairs, remember, as soon as possible—close knitted, plain stitch, rather coarse worsted; and don't forget the hitch, Mrs. Grumbit, don't forget the hitch."

Ah! reader, there are many Mrs. Grumbits in this world requiring *hitches* to be made in their stockings!

At this moment the door burst open. Mrs. Dorothy Grumbit uttered a piercing scream, Mr. Jollyboy dropped his spectacles and sat down on his hat, and Martin Rattler stood before them with the white kitten in his arms.

For a few seconds there was a dead silence, while an expression of puzzled disappointment passed over Mr. Jollyboy's ruddy countenance. At last he said,—

"Is this, madam, the nephew who, you told me a little ago, is not addicted to fighting?"

"Yes," answered the old lady faintly, and covering her eyes with her hands, "that is Martin."

"If my aunt told you that, sir, she told you the truth," said Martin, setting down the blood-stained white kitten, which forthwith began to stretch its limbs and lick itself dry. "I don't ever fight if I can help it, but I couldn't help it to-day."

With a great deal of energy, and a revival of much of his former indignation when he spoke of the kitten's sufferings, Martin recounted all the circumstances of the fight; during the recital of which Mrs. Dorothy Grumbit took his hand in hers and patted it, gazing the while into his swelled visage, and weeping plentifully, but very silently. When he had finished, Mr. Jollyboy shook hands with him, and said he was a trump, at the same time recommending him to go and wash his face. Then he whispered a few words in Mrs. Grumbit's ear, which seemed to give that excellent lady much pleasure; after which he endeavoured to straighten his crushed hat, in which attempt he failed; took his leave, and promised to call again very soon, and went back to the Old Hulk—chuckling.

CHAPTER V.

Martin, being willing to go to sea, goes to sea against his will.

FOUR years rolled away, casting chequered light and shadow over the little village of Ashford in their silent passage—whitening the forelocks of the aged, and strengthening the muscles of the young. Death, too, touched a hearth here and there, and carried desolation to a home; for four years cannot wing their flight without enforcing on us the lesson —which we are so often taught, and yet take so long to learn—that this is not our rest, that here we have no abiding city. Did we but ponder this lesson more frequently and earnestly, instead of making us sad, it would nerve our hearts and hands to fight and work more diligently—to work in the cause of our Redeemer—the only cause that is worth the life-long energy of immortal beings—the great cause that includes all others; and it would teach us to remember that our little day of opportunity will soon be spent, and that the night is at hand in which no man can work.

Four years rolled away, and during this time Martin, having failed to obtain his aunt's consent to his going to sea, continued at school, doing his best to curb the roving spirit that strove within him. Martin was not particularly bright at the dead languages; to the rules of grammar he entertained a rooted aversion; and at history he was inclined to yawn, except when it happened to touch upon the names and deeds of such men as Vasco di Gama and Columbus. But in geography he was perfect; and in arithmetic and book-keeping he was quite a proficient, to the delight of Mrs. Dorothy Grumbit, whose household books he summed up, and to the satisfaction of his fast friend, Mr. Arthur Jollyboy, whose ledgers he was—in that old gentleman's secret resolves—destined to keep.

Martin was now fourteen, broad and strong, and tall for his age. He was the idol of the school— dashing, daring, reckless, and good-natured. There was almost nothing that he would not attempt, and there were very few things that he could not do. He never fought, however—from principle; and his strength and size often saved him from the necessity. But he often prevented other boys from fighting, except when he thought there was good reason for it; then he stood by and saw fair play. There was a strange mixture of philosophical gravity, too, in Martin. As he grew older he became more enthusiastic and less boisterous.

Bob Croaker was still at the school, and was, from prudential motives, a fast friend of Martin. But he bore him a secret grudge, for he could not forget the great fight.

One day Bob took Martin by the arm and said, "I say, Rattler, come with me to Bilton and have some fun among the shipping."

"Well, I don't mind if I do," said Martin. "I'm just in the mood for a ramble, and I'm not expected home till bed-time."

In little more than an hour the two boys were wandering about the dockyards of the sea-port town, and deeply engaged in examining the complicated rigging of the ships. While thus occupied, the clanking of a windlass and the merry, "Yo heave ho! and away she goes," of the sailors, attracted their attention.

"Hallo! there goes the *Firefly*, bound for the South Seas," cried Bob Croaker; "come, let's see her start. I say, Martin, isn't your friend, Barney O'Flannagan, on board?"

"Yes, he is. He tries to get me to go out every voyage, and I wish I could. Come quickly; I want to say good-bye to him before he starts."

"Why don't you run away, Rattler?" inquired Bob, as they hurried round the docks to where the vessel was warping out.

"Because I don't need to. My aunt has given me leave to go if I like; but she says it would break her heart if I do, and I would rather be screwed down to a desk for ever than do that, Bob Croaker."

The vessel, upon the deck of which the two boys now leaped, was a large, heavy-built barque. Her sails were hanging loose, and the captain was giving orders to the men, who had their attention divided between their duties on board and their mothers, wives, and sisters, who still lingered to take a last farewell.

"Now, then, those who don't want to go to sea had better go ashore," roared the captain.

There was an immediate rush to the side.

"I say, Martin," whispered Barney, as he hurried past, "jump down below for'ard; you can go out o' the harbour mouth with us, and get ashore in one o' the shore-boats alongside. They'll not cast off till we're well out. I want to speak to you—"

"Man the fore-top-sail halyards," shouted the first mate.

"Ay, ay, sir-r-r!" and the men sprang to obey. Just then the ship touched on the bar at the mouth of the harbour, and in another moment she was aground.

"There, now, she's hard and fast!" roared the captain, as he stormed about the deck in a paroxysm of rage. But man's rage could avail nothing. They had missed the passage by a few feet, and now they had to wait the fall and rise again of the tide ere they could hope to get off.

In the confusion that followed, Bob Croaker suggested that Martin and he should take one of the punts, or small boats, which hovered round the vessel, and put out to sea, where they might spend the day pleasantly in rowing and fishing.

"Capital!" exclaimed Martin. "Let's go at once. Yonder's a little fellow who will let us have his punt for a few pence. I know him.—Hallo, Tom!"

"Ay, ay," squeaked a boy, who was so small that he could scarcely lift the oar, light though it was, with which he sculled his punt cleverly along.

"Shove alongside, like a good fellow; we want your boat for a little to row out a bit."

"It's a-blowin' too hard," squeaked the small boy, as he ranged alongside. "I'm afeard you'll be blowed out."

"Nonsense!" cried Bob Croaker, grasping the rope which the boy threw to him. "Jump on board, younker; we don't want you to help us, and you're too heavy for ballast. Slip down the side, Martin, and get in while I hold on to the rope. All right? Now I'll follow. Here, shrimp, hold the rope till I'm in, and then cast off. Look alive!"

As Bob spoke, he handed the rope to the little boy, but in doing so let it accidentally slip out of his hand.

"Catch hold o' the main chains, Martin—quick!"

But Martin was too late. The current that swept out of the harbour whirled the light punt away from the ship's side and carried it out seaward. Martin instantly sprang to the oar, and turned the boat's head round. He was a stout and expert rower, and would soon have regained the ship; but the wind increased at the moment, and blew in a squall off shore, which carried him farther out despite his utmost efforts. Seeing that all further attempts were useless, Martin stood up and waved his hand to Bob Croaker, shouting as he did so, "Never mind, Bob, I'll make for the South Point. Run round and meet me, and we'll row back together."

The South Point was a low cape of land which stretched a considerable distance out to sea, about three miles to the southward of Bilton harbour. It formed a large bay, across which, in ordinary weather, a small boat might be rowed in safety. Martin Rattler was well known at the sea-port as a strong and fearless boy, so that no apprehension was entertained for his safety by those who saw him blown away. Bob Croaker immediately started for the Point on foot, a distance of about four miles by land; and the crew of the *Firefly* were so busied with their stranded vessel that they took no notice of the doings of the boys.

But the weather now became more and more stormy. Thick clouds gathered on the horizon. The wind began to blow with steady violence, and shifted a couple of points to the southward, so that Martin found it impossible to keep straight for the Point. Still he worked perseveringly at his single oar, and sculled rapidly over the sea; but as he approached the Point, he soon perceived that no effort of which he was capable could enable him to gain it. But Martin's heart was stout. He strove with all the energy of hope until the Point was passed; and then, turning the head of his little boat towards it, he strove with all the energy of despair, until he fell down exhausted. The wind and tide swept him rapidly out to sea, and when his terrified comrade reached the Point, the little boat was but a speck on the seaward horizon.

Well was it then for Martin Rattler that a friendly heart beat for him on board the *Firefly*. Bob Croaker carried the news to the town, but no one was found daring enough to risk his life out in a boat on that stormy evening. The little punt had been long out of sight ere the news reached them, and the wind had increased to a gale. But Barney O'Flannagan questioned Bob Croaker closely, and took particular note of the point of the compass at which Martin had disappeared; and when the *Firefly* at length got under way, he climbed to the fore-top cross-trees, and stood there scanning the horizon with an anxious eye.

It was getting dark, and a feeling of despair began to creep over the seaman's heart as he gazed round the wide expanse of water, on which nothing was to be seen except the white foam that crested the rising billows.

"Starboard, hard!" he shouted suddenly.

"Starboard it is!" replied the man at the wheel, with prompt obedience.

In another moment Barney slid down the backstay and stood on the deck, while the ship rounded to, and narrowly missed striking a small boat that floated keel up on the water. There was no cry from the boat; and it might have been passed as a mere wreck, had not the lynx-eye of Barney noticed a dark object clinging to it.

"Lower away a boat, lads," cried the Irishman, springing overboard, and the words had scarcely passed his lips when the water closed over his head.

The *Firefly* was hove to, a boat was lowered and rowed towards Barney, whose strong voice guided his shipmates towards him. In less than a quarter of an hour the bold sailor and his young friend Martin Rattler were safe on board, and the ship's head was again turned out to sea.

It was full half-an-hour before Martin was restored to consciousness in the forecastle, to which his deliverer had conveyed him.

"Musha, lad, but ye're booked for the blue wather now, an' no mistake!" said Barney, looking with an expression of deep sympathy at the poor boy, who sat staring before him quite speechless. "The capting 'll not let ye out o' this ship till ye git to the Gould Coast, or some sich place. He couldn't turn back av he wanted iver so much; but he doesn't want to, for he needs a smart lad like you, an' he'll keep you now, for sartin."

Barney sat down by Martin's side and stroked his fair curls, as he sought in his own quaint fashion to console him. But in vain. Martin grew quite desperate as he thought of the misery into which poor Aunt Dorothy Grumbit would be plunged, on learning that he had been swept out to sea in a little boat, and drowned, as she would naturally suppose. In his frenzy he entreated and implored the captain to send him back in the boat, and even threatened to knock out his brains with a handspike if he did not; but the captain smiled, and told him that it was his own fault. He had no business to be putting to sea in a small boat in rough weather; and he might be thankful he wasn't drowned. He wouldn't turn back now for fifty pounds twice told.

At length Martin became convinced that all hope of returning home was gone. He went quietly below, threw himself into one of the sailors' berths, turned his face to the wall, and wept long and bitterly.

CHAPTER VI.

The voyage—A pirate, chase, wreck, and escape.

TIME reconciles a man to almost anything. In the course of time Martin Rattler became reconciled to his fate, and went about the ordinary duties of a cabin-boy on board the *Firefly* just as if he had been appointed to that office in the ordinary way—with the consent of the owners and by the advice of his friends. The captain, Skinflint by name, and as surly an old fellow as ever walked a quarter-deck, agreed to pay him wages "if he behaved well." The steward, under whose immediate authority he was placed, turned out to be a hearty, good-natured young fellow, and was very kind to him. But Martin's great friend was Barney O'Flannagan, the cook, with whom he spent many an hour in the night watches, talking over plans, and prospects, and retrospects, and foreign lands.

As Martin had no clothes except those on his back, which fortunately happened to be new and good,

Barney gave him a couple of blue striped shirts, and made him a jacket, pantaloons, and slippers of canvas; and, what was of much greater importance, taught him how to make and mend the same for himself.

"Ye see, Martin, lad," he said, while thus employed one day, many weeks after leaving port, "it's a great thing, intirely, to be able to help yerself. For my part, I niver travel without my work-box in my pocket."

"Your work-box!" said Martin, laughing.

"Jist so. An' it consists of wan sailmaker's needle, a ball o' twine, and a clasp-knife. Set me down with these before a roll o' canvas and I'll make ye a'most anything."

"You seem to have a turn for everything, Barney," said Martin. "How came you to be a cook?"

"That's more nor I can tell ye, lad. As far as I remimber, I began with murphies, when I was two foot high, in my father's cabin in ould Ireland. But that was on my own account intirely, and not as a purfession; and a sorrowful time I had of it, too, for I was for iver burnin' my fingers promiskiously, and fallin' into the fire ivery day more or less——"

"Stand by to hoist top-gallant-sails!" shouted the captain. "How's her head?"

"South and by east, sir," answered the man at the wheel.

"Keep her away two points. Look alive, lads. Hand me the glass, Martin."

The ship was close-hauled when these abrupt orders were given, battling in the teeth of a stiff breeze, off the coast of South America. About this time several piratical vessels had succeeded in cutting off a number of merchantmen near the coast of Brazil. They had not only taken the valuable parts of their cargoes, but had murdered the crews under circumstances of great cruelty. The ships trading to these regions were, consequently, exceedingly careful to avoid all suspicious craft as much as possible. It was, therefore, with some anxiety that the men watched the captain's face as he examined the strange sail through the telescope.

"A Spanish schooner," muttered the captain, as he shut up the glass with a bang. "I won't trust her. Up with the royals and rig out stun'-sails, Mr. Wilson, (to the mate). Let her fall away, keep her head nor'-west, d'ye hear?"

"Ay, ay, sir."

"Let go the lee braces and square the yards. Look sharp, now, lads. If that blackguard gets hold of us, ye'll have to walk the plank, every man of ye."

In a few minutes the ship's course was completely altered; a cloud of canvas spread out from the yards, and the *Firefly* bounded on her course like a fresh race-horse. But it soon became evident that the heavy barque was no match for the schooner, which crowded sail and bore down at a rate that bade fair to overhaul them in a few hours. The chase continued till evening, when suddenly the look-out at the mast-head shouted, " Land, ho ! "

" Where away ? " cried the captain.

" Right ahead," sang out the man.

" I'll run her ashore sooner than be taken," muttered the captain, with an angry scowl at the schooner, which was now almost within range on the weather quarter, with the dreaded black flag flying at her peak. In a few minutes breakers were descried ahead.

" D'ye see anything like a passage ? " shouted the captain.

" Yes, sir; two points on the weather bow."

At this moment a white cloud burst from the schooner's bow, and a shot, evidently from a heavy gun, came ricochetting over the sea. It was well aimed, for it cut right through the barque's main-mast, just below the yard, and brought the main-top-mast, with all the yards, sails, and gearing above it, down upon the deck. The weight of the wreck, also, carried away the fore-top-mast, and in a single instant the *Firefly* was completely disabled.

"Lower away the boats," cried the captain. "Look alive, now; we'll give them the slip yet. It'll be dark in two minutes."

The captain was right. In tropical regions there is little or no twilight. Night succeeds day almost instantaneously. Before the boats were lowered and the men embarked it was becoming quite dark. The schooner observed the movement, however, and, as she did not dare to venture through the reef in the dark, her boats were also lowered, and the chase was recommenced.

The reef was passed in safety, and now a hard struggle took place, for the shore was still far distant. As it chanced to be cloudy weather, the darkness became intense, and progress could only be guessed at by the sound of the oars; but these soon told too plainly that the boats of the schooner were overtaking those of the barque.

"Pull with a will, lads," cried the captain; "we can't be more than half-a-mile from shore; give way, my hearties."

"Surely, captain, we can fight them; we've most of us got pistols and cutlasses," said one of the men in a sulky tone.

"Fight them!" cried the captain; "they're four times our number, and every man armed to the teeth. If ye don't fancy walking the plank or dancing on nothing at the yard-arm, ye'd better pull away and hold your jaw."

By this time they could just see the schooner's boats in the dim light, about half musket range astern.

"Back you' oars," shouted a stern voice in broken English, "or I blow you out de watter in one oder moment—black-yards!"

This order was enforced by a musket shot, which whizzed over the boat within an inch of the captain's head. The men ceased rowing, and the boats of the pirate ranged close up.

"Now then, Martin," whispered Barney O'Flannagan, who sat at the bow oar, "I'm goin' to swim ashore; jist you slip arter me as quiet as ye can."

"But the sharks!" suggested Martin.

"Bad luck to them," said Barney as he slipped over the side; "they're welcome to me. I'll take my chance. They'll find me mortial tough, anyhow. Come along, lad, look sharp!"

Without a moment's hesitation Martin slid over the gunwale into the sea, and, just as the pirate boats grappled with those of the barque, he and Barney found themselves gliding as silently as otters towards the shore. So quietly had the manœuvre been accomplished, that the men in their own boat were ignorant of their absence. In a few minutes they were beyond the chance of detection.

"Keep close to me, lad," whispered the Irishman. "If we separate in the darkness, we'll niver forgather again. Catch hould o' my shoulder if ye get blowed, and splutter as much as ye like. They can't hear us now, and it'll help to frighten the sharks."

"All right," replied Martin; "I can swim like a cork in such warm water as this. Just go a little slower and I'll do famously."

Thus encouraging each other, and keeping close together, lest they should get separated in the thick darkness of the night, the two friends struck out bravely for the shore.

CHAPTER VII.

Martin and Barney get lost in a great forest, where they see strange and terrible things.

ON gaining the beach, the first thing that Barney did, after shaking himself like a huge Newfoundland dog, was to ascertain that his pistol and cutlass were safe; for, although the former could be of no use in its present condition, still, as he sagaciously remarked, " it was a good thing to have, for they might chance to git powder wan day or other, and the flint would make fire, anyhow." Fortunately the weather was extremely warm; so they were enabled to take off and wring their clothes without much inconvenience, except that in a short time a few adventurous mosquitoes—probably sea-faring ones—came down out of the woods and attacked their bare bodies so vigorously that they were fain to hurry on their clothes again before they were quite dry.

The clouds began to clear away soon after they landed, and the brilliant light of the southern constellations revealed to them dimly the appearance of the coast. It was a low sandy beach skirting the sea and extending back for about a quarter of a mile in the form of a grassy plain, dotted here and there with scrubby underwood. Beyond this was a dark line of forest. The light was not sufficient to enable them to ascertain the appearance of the interior. Barney and Martin now cast about in their minds how they were to spend the night.

"Ye see," said the Irishman, "it's of no use goin' to look for houses, because there's maybe none at all on this coast; an' there's no sayin' but we may fall in with savages—for them parts swarms with them; so we'd better go into the woods an'—"

Barney was interrupted here by a low howl, which proceeded from the woods referred to, and was most unlike any cry they had ever heard before.

"Och, but I'll think better of it. P'r'aps it'll be as well *not* to go into the woods, but to camp where we are."

"I think so too," said Martin, searching about for small twigs and drift-wood with which to make a fire. "There is no saying what sort of wild beasts may be in the forest, so we had better wait till daylight."

A fire was quickly lighted by means of the pistol-flint and a little dry grass, which, when well bruised and put into the pan, caught a spark after one or two attempts, and was soon blown into a flame. But no wood large enough to keep the fire burning for any length of time could be found; so Barney said he would go up to the forest and fetch some. "I'll lave my shoes and socks, Martin, to dry at the fire. See ye don't let them burn."

Traversing the meadow with hasty strides, the bold sailor quickly reached the edge of the forest, where he began to lop off several dead branches from the trees with his cutlass. While thus engaged the howl which had formerly startled him was repeated. "Av I only knowed what ye was," muttered Barney in a serious tone, "it would be some sort o' comfort."

A loud cry of a different kind here interrupted his soliloquy, and soon after the first cry was repeated louder than before.

Clinching his teeth and knitting his brows the perplexed Irishman resumed his work with a desperate resolve not to be again interrupted. But he had miscalculated the strength of his nerves. Albeit as brave a man as ever stepped, when his enemy was before him, Barney was, nevertheless, strongly imbued with superstitious feelings; and the conflict between his physical courage and his mental cowardice produced a species of wild exasperation, which, he often asserted, was very hard to bear. Scarcely had he resumed his work when a bat of enormous size brushed past his nose so noiselessly that it seemed more like a phantom than a reality. Barney had never seen anything of the sort before, and a cold perspiration broke out upon him when he fancied it might be a ghost. Again the bat swept past close to his eyes.

"Musha, but I'll kill ye, ghost or no ghost," he ejaculated, gazing all round into the gloomy depths of the woods with his cutlass uplifted. Instead of flying again in front of him, as he had expected, the bat flew with a whirring noise past his ear. Down came the cutlass with a sudden thwack, cutting deep into the trunk of a small tree, which trembled under the shock, and sent a shower of ripe nuts of a large size down upon the sailor's head. Startled as he was, he sprang backward with a wild cry; then, half ashamed of his groundless fears, he collected the wood he had cut, threw it hastily on his shoulder, and went with a quick step out of the woods. In doing so he put his foot upon the head of a small snake, which wriggled up round his ankle and leg. If there was anything on earth that Barney abhorred and dreaded it was a snake. No sooner did he feel its cold form writhing under his foot, than he uttered a tremendous yell of terror, dropped his bundle of sticks, and fled precipitately to the beach, where he did not halt till he found himself knee-deep in the sea.

"Och, Martin, boy," gasped the affrighted sailor, "it's my belafe that all the evil spirits on arth live in yonder wood; indeed I do."

"Nonsense, Barney," said Martin, laughing; "there are no such things as ghosts; at any rate I'm resolved to face them, for if we don't get some sticks the fire will go out and leave us very comfortless. Come; I'll go up with you."

"Put on yer shoes then, avic, for the sarpints are no ghosts, anyhow, and I'm tould they're pisonous sometimes."

They soon found the bundle of dry sticks that Barney had thrown down, and returning with it to the beach, they speedily kindled a roaring fire, which made them feel quite cheerful. True, they had nothing to eat; but having had a good dinner on board the barque late that afternoon, they were not much in want of food. While they sat thus on the sand of the sea-shore, spreading their hands before the blaze and talking over their strange position, a low rumbling of distant thunder was heard. Barney's countenance instantly fell.

"What's the matter, Barney?" inquired Martin, as he observed his companion gaze anxiously up at the sky.

"Och, it's comin', sure enough."

"And what though it does come?" returned Martin; "we can creep under one of these thick bushes till the shower is past."

"Did ye iver see a thunder-storm in the tropics?" inquired Barney.

"No, never," replied Martin.

"Then, if ye don't want to feel and see it both at wance, come with me as quick as iver ye can."

Barney started up as he spoke, stuck his cutlass and pistol into his belt, and set off towards the woods at a sharp run, followed closely by his wondering companion.

Their haste was by no means unnecessary. Great black clouds rushed up towards the zenith from all points of the compass, and, just as they reached the woods, darkness so thick that it might almost be felt overspread the scene. Then there was a flash of lightning so vivid that it seemed as if a bright day had been created and extinguished in a moment, leaving the darkness ten times more oppressive. It was followed instantaneously by a crash and a prolonged rattle, that sounded as if a universe of solid worlds were rushing into contact overhead and bursting into atoms. The flash was so far useful to the fugitives that it enabled them to observe a many-stemmed tree with dense and heavy foliage, under which they darted. They were just in time, and had scarcely seated themselves among its branches when the rain came down in a way not only that Martin had never seen, but that he had never conceived of before. It fell, as it were, in broad heavy sheets, and its sound was a loud, continuous roar.

The wind soon after burst upon the forest and added to the hideous shriek of elements. The trees bent before it; the rain was whirled and dashed about in water-spouts; and huge limbs were rent from some of the larger trees with a crash like thunder, and swept far away into the forest. The very earth trembled and seemed terrified at the dreadful conflict going on above. It seemed to the two friends as if the end of the world were come; and they could do nothing but cower among the branches of the tree and watch the storm in silence, while they felt, in a way they had never before experienced, how utterly helpless they were and unable to foresee or avert the many dangers by which they were surrounded, and how absolutely dependent they were on God for protection.

For several hours the storm continued. Then it ceased as suddenly as it had begun, and the bright stars again shone down upon the peaceful scene.

When it was over, Martin and his comrade descended the tree and endeavoured to find their way back to the beach. But this was no easy matter. The haste with which they had run into the woods, and the confusion of the storm, had made them uncertain in which direction it lay; and the more they tried to get out, the deeper they penetrated into the forest. At length, wearied with fruitless wandering and stumbling about in the dark, they resolved to spend the night where they were. Coming to a place which was more open than usual, and where they could see a portion of the starry sky overhead, they sat down on a dry spot under the shelter of a spreading tree, and, leaning their backs against the trunk, very soon fell sound asleep.

CHAPTER VIII.

An enchanting land—An uncomfortable bed, and a queer breakfast—Many surprises and a few frights, together with a notable discovery.

"I'VE woked in paradise!"

Such was the exclamation that aroused Martin Rattler on the morning after his landing on the coast of South America. It was uttered by Barney O'Flannagan, who lay at full length on his back, his head propped up by a root of the tree under which they had slept, and his eyes staring right before him with an expression of concentrated amazement. When Martin opened his eyes, he too was struck dumb with surprise. And well might they gaze with astonishment; for the last ray of departing daylight on the night before had flickered over the open sea, and now the first gleam of returning sunshine revealed to them the magnificent forests of Brazil.

Yes, well might they gaze and gaze again in boundless admiration; for the tropical sun shone down on a scene of dazzling and luxuriant vegetation, so resplendent that it seemed to them the realization of a fairy tale. Plants and shrubs and flowers were there of the most curious and brilliant description, and of which they neither knew the uses nor the names. Majestic trees were there with foliage of every shape and size and hue—some with stems twenty feet in circumference, others more slender in form, straight and tall, and some twisted in a bunch together and rising upwards like fluted pillars; a few had buttresses, or natural planks, several feet broad, ranged all round their trunks, as if to support them; while many bent gracefully beneath the load of their clustering fruit and heavy foliage. Orange-trees with their ripe fruit shone in the sunbeams like gold. Stately palms rose above the surrounding trees and waved their feathery plumes in the air, and bananas with broad enormous leaves rustled in the breeze and cast a cool shadow on the ground.

Well might they gaze in great surprise, for all these curious and beautiful trees were surrounded by and entwined in the embrace of luxuriant and remarkable climbing-plants. The parasitic vanilla with its star-like blossoms crept up their trunks and along their branches, where it hung in graceful festoons, or drooped back again almost to the ground. So rich and numerous were these creepers that in many cases they killed the strong giants whom they embraced so lovingly. Some of them hung from the tree-tops like stays from the masts of a ship, and many of them mingled their brilliant flowers so closely with the leaves that the climbing-plants and their supporters could not be distinguished from each other, and it seemed as though the trees themselves had become gigantic flowering shrubs.

Birds, too, were there in myriads—and such birds! Their feathers were green and gold and scarlet and yellow and blue—fresh and bright and brilliant as the sky beneath which they were nurtured. The great toucan, with a beak nearly as big as his body, flew clumsily from stem to stem. The tiny, delicate humming-birds, scarce larger than bees, fluttered from flower to flower and spray to spray like points of brilliant green. But they were irritable, passionate little creatures, these lovely things, and quarrelled with each other and fought like very wasps! Enormous butterflies, with wings of deep metallic blue, shot past or hovered in the air like gleams of light; and green paroquets swooped from tree to tree, and chattered joyfully over their morning meal.

Well might they gaze with wonder, and smile too with extreme merriment, for monkeys stared at them from between the leaves with expressions of undisguised amazement, and bounded away shrieking and chattering in consternation, swinging from branch to branch with incredible speed, and not scrupling to use each other's tails to swing by when occasion offered. Some were big and red and ugly—as ugly as you can possibly imagine, with blue faces and fiercely grinning teeth; others were delicately formed, and sad of countenance, as if they were for ever bewailing the loss of near and dear relations, and could by no means come at consolation; and some were small and pretty, with faces no bigger than a halfpenny. As a general rule, it seemed to Barney, the smaller the monkey the longer the tail.

Yes, well might they gaze and gaze again in surprise and in excessive admiration; and well might Barney O'Flannagan—under the circumstances, with such sights and sounds around him, and the delightful odours of myrtle trees and orange blossoms and the Cape jessamine stealing up his nostrils—deem himself the tenant of another world, and evince his conviction of the fact in that memorable expression— " I've woked in paradise!"

But Barney began to find "paradise" not quite so comfortable as it ought to be; for when he tried to get up he found his bones pained and stiff from sleeping in damp clothes, and, moreover, his face was very much swelled, owing to the myriads of mosquitoes which had supped of it during the night.

"Arrah, then, *won't* ye be done?" he cried angrily, giving his face a slap that killed at least two or three hundred of his tormentors. But thousands more attacked him instantly, and he soon found out—what every one finds out sooner or later in hot climates—that *patience* is one of the best remedies for mosquito bites. He also discovered shortly afterwards that smoke is not a bad remedy, in connection with patience.

"What are we to have for breakfast, Barney?" inquired Martin, as he rose and yawned and stretched his limbs.

"Help yersilf to what ye plase," said Barney, with a polite bow, waving his hand round him, as if the forest were his private property and Martin Rattler his honoured guest.

"Well, I vote for oranges," said Martin, going towards a tree which was laden with ripe fruit.

"An' I'll try plums, by way of variety," added his companion.

In a few minutes several kinds of fruit and nuts were gathered and spread at the foot of the tree under which they had reposed. Then Barney proceeded to kindle a fire; not that he had anything to cook, but he said it looked sociable-like, and the smoke would keep off the flies. The operation, however, was by no means easy. Everything had been soaked by the rain of the previous night, and a bit of dry grass could scarcely be found. At length he procured a little, and by rubbing it in the damp gunpowder which he had extracted from his pistol, and drying it in the sun, he formed a sort of tinder that caught fire after much persevering effort.

Some of the fruits they found to be good, others bad. The good they ate, the bad they threw away. After their frugal fare they felt much refreshed, and then began to talk of what they should do.

"We can't live here with parrots and monkeys, you know," said Martin; "we must try to find a village or town of some sort, or get to the coast, and then we shall perhaps meet with a ship."

"True, lad," replied Barney, knitting his brows and looking extremely sagacious; "the fact is, since neither of us knows nothing about anything, or the way to any place, my advice is to walk straight for'ard till we come to something."

"So think I," replied Martin; "therefore the sooner we set off the better."

Having no luggage to pack and no arrangements of any kind to make, the two friends rose from their primitive breakfast-table, and walked away straight before them into the forest.

All that day they travelled patiently forward, conversing pleasantly about the various and wonderful trees and flowers and animals they met with by the way; but no signs were discovered that indicated the presence of man. Towards evening, however, they fell upon a track or footpath, which discovery rejoiced them much; and here, before proceeding farther, they sat down to eat a little more fruit—which indeed they had done several times during the day. They walked nearly thirty miles that day without seeing a human being; but they met with many strange and beautiful birds and beasts, some of which were of so fierce an aspect that they would have been very glad to have had guns to defend themselves with. Fortunately, however, all the animals seemed to be much more afraid of them than they were of the animals, so they travelled in safety. Several times during the course of the day they saw snakes and serpents, which glided away into the jungle on their approach, and could not be overtaken, although Barney made repeated darts at them, intending to attack them with his cutlass, which assaults always proved fruitless.

Once they were charged by a herd of peccaries—a species of pig or wild hog—from which they escaped by jumping actively to one side; but the peccaries turned and rushed at them again, and it was only by springing up the branches of a neighbouring tree that they escaped their fury. These peccaries are the fiercest and most dauntless animals in the forests of Brazil. They do not know what fear is; they will rush in the face of anything; and, unlike all other animals, are quite indifferent to the report of fire-arms. Their bodies are covered with long bristles, resembling very much the quills of the porcupine.

As the evening drew on, the birds and beasts and the innumerable insects, that had kept up a perpetual noise during the day, retired to rest; and then the nocturnal animals began to creep out of their holes and go about. Huge vampire-bats, one of which had given Barney such a fright the night before, flew silently past them, and the wild howlings commenced again. They now discovered that one of the most dismal of the howls proceeded from a species of monkey, at which discovery Martin laughed very much, and rallied his companion on being so easily frightened; but Barney gladly joined in the laugh against himself, for, to say truth, he felt quite relieved and light-hearted at discovering that his ghosts were converted into bats and monkeys!

There was one roar, however, which, when they

heard it ever and anon, gave them considerable uneasiness.

"D'ye think there's lions in them parts?" inquired Barney, glancing with an expression of regret at his empty pistol, and laying his hand on the hilt of his cutlass.

"I think not," replied Martin, in a low tone of voice. "I have read in my school geography that there are tigers of some sort—jaguars or ounces, I think they are called—but there are no——"

Martin's speech was cut short by a terrific roar which rang through the woods, and the next instant a magnificent jaguar, or South American tiger, bounded on to the track a few yards in advance, and, wheeling round, glared fiercely at the travellers. It seemed, in the uncertain light, as if his eyes were two balls of living fire. Though not so large as the royal Bengal tiger of India, this animal was nevertheless of immense size, and had a very ferocious aspect. His roar was so sudden and awful, and his appearance so unexpected, that the blood was sent thrilling back into the hearts of the travellers, who stood rooted to the spot, absolutely unable to move. This was the first large animal of the cat kind that either of them had seen in all the terrible majesty of its wild condition; and, for the first time, Martin and his friend felt that awful sensation of dread that will assail even the bravest heart when a new species of imminent danger is suddenly presented. It is said that no animal can withstand the steady gaze of a human eye, and many travellers in wild countries have proved this to be a fact. On the present occasion our adventurers stared long and steadily at the wild creature before them, from a mingled feeling of surprise and horror. In a few seconds the jaguar showed signs of being disconcerted. It turned its head from side to side slightly, and dropped its eyes, as if to avoid their gaze. Then turning slowly and stealthily round, it sprang with a magnificent bound into the jungle and disappeared.

Both Martin and Barney heaved a deep sigh of relief.

"What a mercy it did not attack us!" said the former, wiping the cold perspiration from his forehead. "We should have had no chance against such a terrible beast with a cutlass, I fear."

"True, boy, true," replied his friend gravely; "it would have been little better than a penknife in the ribs o' sich a cratur. I niver thought that it was in the power o' man or baste to put me in sich a fright; but the longer we live we learn, boy."

Barney's disposition to make light of everything

was thoroughly subdued by this incident, and he felt none of his usual inclination to regard all that he saw in the Brazilian forests with a comical eye. The danger they had escaped was too real and terrible, and their almost unarmed condition too serious, to be lightly esteemed. For the next hour or two he continued to walk by Martin's side either in total silence or in earnest, grave conversation; but by degrees these feelings wore off, and his buoyant spirits gradually returned.

The country over which they had passed during the day was of a mingled character. At one time they traversed a portion of dark forest, heavy and choked up with the dense and gigantic foliage peculiar to those countries that lie near to the equator; then they emerged from this upon what to their eyes seemed most beautiful scenery—mingled plain and woodland—where the excessive brilliancy and beauty of the tropical vegetation was brought to perfection by exposure to the light of the blue sky and the warm rays of the sun. In such lovely spots they travelled more slowly and rested more frequently, enjoying to the full the sight of the gaily-coloured birds and insects that fluttered busily around them, and the delicious perfume of the flowers that decked the ground and clambered up the trees. At other times they came to plains, or *campos*, as they are termed, where there were no trees at all, and few shrubs, and where the grass was burned brown and dry by the sun. Over such they hurried as quickly as they could; and fortunately, where they chanced to travel, such places were neither numerous nor extensive, although in some districts of Brazil there are campos hundreds of miles in extent.

A small stream meandered through the forest, and enabled them to refresh themselves frequently, which was very fortunate; for the heat, especially towards noon, became extremely intense, and they could not have existed without water. So great, indeed, was the heat about mid-day that, by mutual consent, they resolved to seek the cool shade of a spreading tree, and try to sleep if possible. At this time they learned, to their surprise, that all animated nature did likewise, and sought repose at noon. God had implanted in the breast of every bird and insect in that mighty forest an instinct which taught it to rest and find refreshment during the excessive heat of mid-day; so that, during the space of two or three hours, not a thing with life was seen, and not a sound was heard. Even the troublesome mosquitoes, so active at all other times, day and night, were silent now. The change was very great and striking, and difficult for those who have not observed it to comprehend. All the forenoon, screams, and cries, and croaks, and grunts, and whistles ring out through the woods incessantly; while, if you listen attentively, you hear the low, deep, and never-ending buzz and hum of millions upon millions of insects, that dance in the air and creep on every leaf and blade upon the ground. About noon all this is hushed. The hot rays of the sun beat perpendicularly down upon what seems a vast untenanted solitude, and not a single chirp breaks the death-like stillness of the great forest, with the solitary exception of the metallic note of the uruponga, or bell-bird, which seems to mount guard when all the rest of the world has gone to sleep. As the afternoon approaches they all wake up, refreshed by their siesta, active and lively as fairies, and ready for another spell of work and another deep-toned noisy chorus.

The country through which our adventurers travelled, as evening approached, became gradually more hilly, and their march consequently more toilsome. They were just about to give up all thought of proceeding farther that night when, on reaching the summit of a little hill, they beheld a bright red light shining at a considerable distance in the valley beyond. With light steps and hearts full of hope they descended the hill and hastened towards it.

CHAPTER IX.

The hermit.

IT was now quite dark, and the whole country seemed alive with fire-flies. These beautiful little insects sat upon the trees and bushes, spangling them as with living diamonds, and flew about in the air like little wandering stars. Barney had seen them before, in the West Indies; but Martin had only heard of them, and his delight and amazement at their extreme brilliancy were very great. Although he was naturally anxious to reach the light in the valley, in the hope that it might prove to proceed from some cottage, he could not refrain from stopping once or twice to catch these lovely creatures; and when he succeeded in doing so, and placed one on the palm of his hand, the light emitted from it was more brilliant than that of a small taper, and much more beautiful, for it was of a bluish colour, and very intense—more like the light reflected from a jewel than a flame of fire. He could have read a book by means of it quite easily

In half-an-hour they drew near to the light, which they found proceeded from the window of a small cottage or hut.

"Whist, Martin," whispered Barney, as they approached the hut on tiptoe; "there may be savages into it, an' there's no sayin' what sort o' craturs they are in them parts."

When about fifty yards distant, they could see through the open window into the room where the light burned; and what they beheld there was well calculated to fill them with surprise. On a rude wooden chair, at a rough unpainted table, a man was seated, with his head resting on his hand and his eyes fixed intently on a book. Owing to the distance, and the few leaves and branches that intervened between them and the hut, they could not observe him very distinctly. But it was evident that he was a large and strong man, a little past the prime of life. The hair of his head and beard was black and bushy, and streaked with silver-gray. His face was massive, and of a dark olive complexion, with an expression of sadness on it, strangely mingled with stern gravity. His broad shoulders—and, indeed, his whole person—were enveloped in the coarse folds of a long gown or robe, gathered in at the waist with a broad band of leather.

The room in which he sat—or rather the hut, for there was but one room in it—was destitute of all furniture, except that already mentioned, besides one or two roughly-formed stools; but the walls were completely covered with strange-looking implements and trophies of the chase; and in a corner lay a confused pile of books, some of which were, from their appearance, extremely ancient. All this the benighted wanderers observed as they continued to approach cautiously on tiptoe. So cautious did they become as they drew near and came within the light of the lamp, that Barney at length attempted to step over his own shadow for fear of making a noise, and in doing so tripped and fell with considerable noise through a hedge of prickly shrubs that encircled the strange man's dwelling.

The hermit—for such he appeared to be—betrayed no symptom of surprise or fear at the sudden sound, but rising quietly though quickly from his seat, took down a musket that hung on the wall, and stepping to the open door demanded sternly, in the Portuguese language, "Who goes there?"

"Arrah, then, if ye'd help a fellow-cratur to rise, instead o' talkin' gibberish like that, it would be more to yer credit!" exclaimed the Irishman, as he scrambled to his feet and presented himself, along with Martin, at the hermit's door.

A peculiar smile lighted up the man's features as he retreated into the hut, and invited the strangers to enter.

"Come in," said he, in good English, although with a slightly foreign accent. "I am most happy to see you. You are English. I know the voice and the language very well. Lived among them once, but long time past now—very long. Have not seen one of you for many years."

With many such speeches and much expression of good-will the hospitable hermit invited Martin and his companion to sit down at his rude table, on which he quickly spread several plates of ripe and dried fruits, a few cakes, and a jar of excellent honey, with a stone bottle of cool water. When they were busily engaged with these viands, he began to make inquiries as to where his visitors had come from.

"We've comed from the sae," replied Barney, as he devoted himself to a magnificent pine-apple. "Och, but yer victuals is mighty good, Mister—what's yer name?—'ticklerly to them that's a'most starvin'."

"The fact is," said Martin, "our ship has been taken by pirates, and we two swam ashore and lost ourselves in the woods; and now we have stumbled upon your dwelling, friend, which is a great comfort."

"Hoigh, an' that's true," sighed Barney, as he finished the last slice of the pine-apple.

They now explained to their entertainer all the circumstances attending the capture of the *Firefly*, and their subsequent adventures and vicissitudes in the forest; all of which Barney detailed in a most graphic manner, and to all of which their new friend listened with grave attention and unbroken silence. When they had concluded, he said,—

"Very good. You have seen much in very short time. Perhaps you shall see more by-and-by. For the present you will go to rest, for you must be fatigued. I will *think* to-night—to-morrow I will *speak*."

"An' if I may make so bould," said Barney, glancing with a somewhat rueful expression round the hard earthen floor of the hut, "whereabouts may I take the liberty o' sleepin'?"

The hermit replied by going to a corner, whence, from beneath a heap of rubbish, he dragged two hammocks, curiously wrought in a sort of light network. These he slung across the hut, at one end, from wall to wall, and throwing a sheet or coverlet into each, he turned with a smile to his visitors,—

"Behold your beds! I wish you a very good sleep—adios!"

So saying, this strange individual sat down at the table, and was soon as deeply engaged with his large book as if he had suffered no interruption; while Martin and Barney, having gazed gravely and abstractedly at him for five minutes, turned and smiled to each other, jumped into their hammocks, and were soon buried in deep slumber.

CHAPTER X.

An enemy in the night—The vampire bat—The hermit discourses on strange, and curious, and interesting things.

NEXT morning Martin Rattler awoke with a feeling of lightness in his head and a sensation of extreme weakness pervading his entire frame. Turning his head round to the right he observed that a third hammock was slung across the farther end of the hut, which was, no doubt, that in which the hermit had passed the night. But it was empty now. Martin did not require to turn his head to the other side to see if Barney O'Flannagan was there, for that worthy individual made his presence known, for a distance of at least sixty yards all round the outside of the hut, by means of his nose, which he was in the habit of using as a trumpet when asleep. It was as well that Martin did not require to look round, for he found, to his surprise, that he had scarcely strength to do so. While he was wondering in a dreamy sort of manner what could be the matter with him, the hermit entered the hut bearing a small deer upon his shoulders. Resting his gun in a corner of the room, he advanced to Martin's hammock.

"My boy!" he exclaimed in surprise, "what is wrong with you?"

"I'm sure I don't know," said Martin faintly. "I think there is something wet about my feet."

Turning up the sheet, he found that Martin's feet were covered with blood! For a few seconds the hermit growled forth a number of apparently very pithy sentences in Portuguese, in a deep guttural voice, which awakened Barney with a start. Springing from his hammock with a bound like a tiger, he exclaimed, "Och! ye blackguard, would ye murther the boy before me very nose?" and seizing the hermit in his powerful grasp, he would infallibly have hurled him, big though he was, through his own doorway, had not Martin cried out, "Stop, stop, Barney! It's all right; he's done nothing," on hearing which the Irishman loosened his hold, and turned towards his friend.

"What's the matter, honey?" said Barney in a soothing tone of voice, as a mother might address her infant son.

The hermit, whose composure had not been in the slightest degree disturbed, here said,—

"The poor child has been sucked by a vampire bat."

"Ochone!" groaned Barney, sitting down on the table, and looking at his host with a face of horror.

"Yes, these are the worst animals in Brazil for sucking the blood of men and cattle. I find it quite impossible to keep my mules alive, they are so bad."

Barney groaned.

"They have killed two cows which I tried to keep here, and one young horse—a foal you call him, I think; and now I have no cattle remaining, they are so bad."

Barney groaned again, and the hermit went on to enumerate the wicked deeds of the vampire bats, while he applied poultices of certain herbs to Martin's toe, in order to check the bleeding, and then bandaged it up; after which he sat down to relate to his visitors the manner in which the bat carries on its bloody operations. He explained, first of all, that the vampire bats are so large and ferocious that they often kill horses and cattle by sucking their blood out. Of course they cannot do this at one meal, but they attack the poor animals again and again, and the blood continues to flow from the wounds they make long afterwards, so that the creatures attacked soon grow weak and die. They attack men, too, as Martin knew to his cost; and they usually fix upon the toes and other extremities. So gentle are they in their operations, that sleepers frequently do not feel the puncture which they make, it is supposed, with the sharp-hooked nail of their thumb; and the unconscious victim knows nothing of the enemy who has been draining his blood until he awakens, faint and exhausted, in the morning.

Moreover, the hermit told them that these vampire bats have very sharp, carnivorous teeth, besides a tongue which is furnished with the curious organs by which they suck the life-blood of their victims; that they have a peculiar, leaf-like, overhanging lip; and that he had a stuffed specimen of a bat that measured no less than two feet across the expanded wings, from tip to tip.

"Och, the blood-thirsty spalpeen!" exclaimed Barney, as he rose and crossed the room to examine the bat in question, which was nailed against the wall. "Bad luck to them; they've ruined Martin intirely."

"Oh no," remarked the hermit with a smile. "It will do the boy much good the loss of the blood, much good, and he will not be sick at all to-morrow."

"I'm glad to hear you say so," said Martin; "for

it would be a great bore to be obliged to lie here when I've so many things to see. In fact I feel better already, and if you will be so kind as to give me a little breakfast I shall be quite well."

While Martin was speaking, the obliging hermit—who, by the way, was now habited in a loose, short hunting-coat of brown cotton—spread a plentiful repast upon his table, to which, having assisted Martin to get out of his hammock, they all proceeded to do ample justice; for the travellers were very hungry after the fatigue of the previous day, and as for the hermit, he looked like a man whose appetite was always sharp set, and whose food agreed with him.

They had cold meat of several kinds, and a hot steak of venison just killed that morning, which the hermit cooked while his guests were engaged with the other viands. There was also excellent coffee, and superb cream, besides cakes made of a species of coarse flour or meal, fruits of various kinds, and very fine honey.

"Arrah! ye've the hoith o' livin' here!" cried Barney, smacking his lips as he held out his plate for another supply of a species of meat which resembled chicken in tenderness and flavour. "What sort o' bird or baste may that be, now, av I may ask ye, Mister—what's yer name?"

"My name is Carlos," replied the hermit gravely; "and this is the flesh of the armadillo."

"Arma—what—o?" inquired Barney.

"Arma*dillo*," repeated the hermit. "He is very good to eat, but very difficult to catch. He digs down so fast we cannot catch him, and must smoke him out of his hole."

"Have you many cows?" inquired Martin, as he replenished his cup with coffee.

"Cows?" echoed the hermit; "I have got no cows."

"Where do you get such capital cream, then?" asked Martin in surprise.

The hermit smiled. "Ah, my friends, that cream has come from a very curious cow. It is from a cow that grows in the ground."

"Grows!" ejaculated his guests.

"Yes, he grows. I will show him to you one day."

The hermit's broad shoulders shook with a quiet internal laugh. "I will explain a little of that you behold on my table. The coffee I get from the trees. There are plenty of them here. Much money is made in Brazil by the export of coffee—very much. The cakes are made from the mandioca root, which I grow near my house. The root is dried and ground into flour, which, under the general name *farina*, is used all over the country. It is almost the only food used by the Indians and Negroes."

"Then there are Injins and Niggers here, are there?" inquired Barney.

"Yes, a great many. Most of the Negroes are slaves; some of the Indians too; and the people who are descended from the Portuguese who came and took the country long ago, they are the masters.— Well, the honey I get in holes in the trees. There are different kinds of honey here; some of it is *sour* honey. And the fruits and roots, the plantains, and bananas, and yams, and cocoa-nuts, and oranges, and plums, all grow in the forest, and much more besides, which you will see for yourselves if you stay long here."

"It's a quare country, intirely," remarked Barney, as he wiped his mouth and heaved a sigh of contentment. Then, drawing his hand over his chin, he looked earnestly in the hermit's face, and, with a peculiar twinkle in his eye, said,—

"I s'pose ye couldn't favour me with the lind of a raazor, could ye?"

"No, my friend; I never use that foolish weapon."

"Ah, well, as there's only monkeys and jaguars, and sich like to see me, it don't much signify; but my mustaches is gitin' mighty long, for I've been two weeks already without a shave."

Martin laughed heartily at the grave, anxious expression of his comrade's face. "Never mind, Barney," he said, "a beard and moustache will improve you vastly. Besides, they will be a great protection against mosquitoes; for you are such a hairy monster, that when they grow nothing of your face will be exposed except your eyes and cheek-bones. And now," continued Martin, climbing into his hammock again and addressing the hermit, "since you won't allow me to go out a-hunting to-day, I would like very much if you would tell me something more about this strange country."

"An' maybe," suggested Barney modestly, "ye won't object to tell us something about yersilf—how you came for to live in this quare, solitary kind of a way."

The hermit looked gravely from one to the other, and stroked his beard. Drawing his rude chair towards the door of the hut, he folded his arms, and crossed his legs, and gazed dreamily forth upon the rich landscape. Then, glancing again at his guests, he said slowly, "Yes, I will do what you ask—I will tell you my story."

"An' if I might make so bould as to inquire," said

Barney, with a deprecatory smile, while he drew a short black pipe from his pocket, "have ye got sich a thing as 'baccy in them parts?"

The hermit rose, and going to a small box which stood in a corner, returned with a quantity of cut tobacco in one hand, and a cigar not far short of a foot long in the other! In a few seconds the cigar was going in full force, like a factory chimney; and the short black pipe glowed like a miniature furnace, while its owner seated himself on a low stool, crossed his arms on his breast, leaned his back against the door-post, and smiled, as only an Irishman can smile under such circumstances. The smoke soon formed a thick cloud, which effectually drove the mosquitoes out of the hut, and through which Martin, lying in his hammock, gazed out upon the sunlit orange and coffee trees, and tall palms with their rich festoons of creeping plants, and sweet-scented flowers, that clambered over and round the hut and peeped in at the open door and windows, while he listened to the hermit, who continued for at least ten minutes to murmur slowly, between the puffs of his cigar, "Yes, I will do it—I will tell you my story."

CHAPTER XL.

The hermit's story.

"MY ancestors," began the hermit, "were among the first to land upon Brazil, after the country was taken possession of in the name of the King of Portugal, in the year 1500. In the first year of the century, Vincent Yanez Pinçon, a companion of the famed Columbus, discovered Brazil; and in the next year, Pedro Alvarez Cabral, a Portuguese commander, took possession of it in the name of the King of Portugal. In 1503, Americus Vespucius discovered the Bay of All Saints, and took home a cargo of Brazil-wood, monkeys, and parrots; but no permanent settlement was effected upon the shores of the new continent, and the rich treasures of this great country remained for some years longer buried and unknown to man, for the wild Indians who lived here knew not their value.

"It was on a dark and stormy night in the year 1510. A group of swarthy and naked savages encircled a small fire on the edge of the forest on the east coast of Brazil. The spot where their watchfire was kindled is now covered by the flourishing city of Bahia. At that time it was a wilderness. Before them stretched the noble bay which is now termed *Bahia de Todos Santos*—All Saints' Bay.

"The savages talked earnestly and with excited looks as they stood upon the shore, for the memory of the wondrous ships of the white men that had visited them a few years before was deeply engraven on their minds; and now, in the midst of the howling storm, another ship was seen approaching their land. It was a small vessel, shattered and tempest-tossed, that drove into the Bahia de Todos Santos on that stormy night. Long had it battled with the waves of the Atlantic, and the brave hearts that manned it had remained stanch to duty and strong in hope, remembering the recent glorious example of Columbus. But the storm was fierce and the bark was frail. The top-masts were broken and the sails rent; and worst of all, just as land hove in sight and cheered the drooping spirits of the crew, a tremendous wave dashed upon the ship's stern and carried away the rudder.

"As they drove helplessly before the gale towards the shore, the naked savages crowded down upon the beach and gazed in awe and astonishment at the mysterious ship. A few of them had seen the vessels of Americus Vespucius and Cabral. The rumour of the white men and their floating castles had been wafted far and wide along the coast and into the interior of Brazil, and with breathless wonder the natives had listened to the strange account. But now the vision was before them in reality. On came the floating castle, the white foam dashing from her bows, and the torn sails and ropes flying from her masts, as she surged over the billows and loomed through the driving spray.

"It was a grand sight to see that ship dashing straight towards the shore at fearful speed; and those who looked on seemed to be impressed with a vague feeling that she had power to spring upon the strand and continue her swift career through the forest, as she had hitherto cleft her passage through the sea. As she approached, the savages shrank back in fear. Suddenly her frame trembled with a mighty shock. A terrible cry was borne to land by the gale, and all her masts went overboard. A huge wave lifted the vessel on its crest and flung her farther on the shore, where she remained firmly fixed, while the waves dashed in foam around her and soon began to break her up. Ere this happened, however, a rope was thrown ashore, and fastened to a rock by the natives. By means of this the crew were saved. But it would have been well for these bold navigators of Portugal if they had perished in the stormy sea, for they were spared by the ocean only to be murdered by the wild savages on whose shore they had been cast.

"All were slain save one—Diego Alvarez Carreo, the captain of the ship. Before grasping the rope by which he reached the shore, he thrust several cartridges into his bosom and caught up a loaded musket. Wrapping the lock in several folds of cloth to keep it dry, he slid along the rope and gained the beach in safety. Here he was seized by the natives, and would no doubt have been barbarously slain with his unfortunate companions, but being a very powerful man he dashed aside the foremost, and breaking through their ranks, rushed towards the wood. The fleet savages, however, overtook him in an instant, and were about to seize him when a young Indian woman interposed between them and their victim. This girl was the chief's daughter, and respect for her rank induced them to hesitate for a moment; but in another instant the Portuguese captain was surrounded. In the scuffle that ensued his musket exploded, but fortunately wounded no one. Instantly the horrified savages fled in all directions, leaving Carreo alone!

"The captain was quick-witted. He knew that among hundreds of savages it was madness to attempt either to fight or to fly, and the happy effect of the musket explosion induced him to adopt another course of action. He drew himself up proudly to his full height, and beckoned the savages to return. This they did, casting many glances of fear at the dreaded musket. Going up to one who, from his bearing and ornaments, seemed to be a chief, Carreo laid his musket on the sand, and, stepping over it so that he left it behind him, held out his hand frankly to the chief. The savage looked at him in surprise, and suffered the captain to take his hand and pat it; after which he began to examine the stranger's dress with much curiosity. Seeing that their chief was friendly to the white man, the other savages hurried him to the camp-fire, where he soon stripped off his wet clothes and ate the food which they put before him. Thus Diego Carreo was spared.

"Next day, the Indians lined the beach and collected the stores of the wrecked vessel. While thus employed, Carreo shot a gull with his musket, which so astonished the natives that they regarded him with fear and respect amounting almost to veneration. A considerable quantity of powder and shot was saved from the wreck, so that the captain was enabled to keep his ascendency over the ignorant natives; and at length he became a man of great importance in the tribe, and married the daughter of the chief. He went by the name of *Caramuru*—' the man of fire.' This man founded the city of Bahia.

"The coasts of Brazil began soon after this to be settled in various places by the Portuguese, who, however, were much annoyed by the Spaniards, who claimed a share in the rich prize. The Dutch and English also formed settlements, but the Portuguese still retained possession of the country, and continued to prosper. Meanwhile Diego Caramuru, 'the man of fire,' had a son who in course of time became a prosperous settler; and as his sons grew up he trained them to become cultivators of the soil and traders in the valuable products of the New World. He took a piece of ground, far removed from the spot where his father had been cast ashore, and a short distance in the interior of the country. Here the eldest sons of the family dwelt, laboured, and died, for many generations.

"In the year 1808 Portugal was invaded by Napoleon Buonaparte, and the sovereign of that kingdom, John VI., fled to Brazil, accompanied by his court and a large body of emigrants. The king was warmly received by the Brazilians, and immediately set about improving the condition of the country. He threw open its ports to all nations, freed the land from all marks of colonial dependence, established newspapers, made the press free, and did everything to promote education and industry. But although much was done, the good was greatly hindered, especially in the inland districts, by the vice, ignorance, and stupidity of many of the Roman Catholic priests, who totally neglected their duties—which, indeed, they were incompetent to perform—and in many instances were no better than miscreants in disguise, teaching the people vice instead of virtue.

"Foremost among the priests who opposed advancement was a descendant of the 'man of fire.' Padre Caramuru dwelt for some years with an English merchant in the capital of Brazil, Rio de Janeiro. The padre was not an immoral man, but he was a fiery bigot, and fiercely opposed everything that tended to advance the education of the people. This he did, firmly believing that education was dangerous to the lower orders. His church taught him, too, that the Bible was a dangerous book, and whenever a copy fell into his hands he immediately destroyed it. During the disturbances that took place after the time of King John's departure for Portugal, and just before Brazil became an independent state under his son, the Emperor Don Pedro I., Padre Caramuru lost a beloved and only brother. He was quite a youth, and had joined the army only a few months previously at the desire of his elder brother the padre, who was so overwhelmed by the blow that he ceased to take an active part in church or political affairs, and buried himself in a retired part of his native valley. Here he sought relief and comfort in the study of the beauties of nature by which he was surrounded, but found none. Then he turned his mind to the doctrines of his church, and took pleasure in verifying them from the Bible. But as he proceeded he found, to his great surprise, that these doctrines were, many of them, not to be found there; nay, further, that some of them were absolutely contradicted by the Word of God.

"Padre Caramuru had been in the habit of commanding his people not to listen to the Bible when any one offered to read it; but in the Bible itself he found these words, 'Search the Scriptures.' He had been in the habit of praying to the Virgin Mary, and begging her to intercede with God for him; but in the Bible he found these words: 'There is one mediator between God and men, the man Christ Jesus.' These things perplexed him much. But while he was thus searching, as it were, for silver, the ignorant padre found gold! He found that he did not require to *work* for salvation, but to *ask* for it. He discovered that the atonement had been made once for all by Jesus Christ, the Lamb of God; and he read with a thrilling heart these words: 'God so loved the world, that he gave his only begotten Son, that whosoever believeth in him should not perish, but have everlasting life.'

"Long and earnestly did the padre ponder these words and pray over them; and gradually the Holy Spirit enlightened his mind, and he saw how hateful that system was which could forbid or discourage the reading of the blessed Word of God. He soon resolved to forsake the priesthood. But when he had done so, he knew not what to turn his hand to. He had no one like-minded to consult with, and he felt that it was wrong to eat the bread of idleness. Being thus uncertain what to do, he resolved in the meantime to carry goods into the interior of the country and offer them for sale. The land round his dwelling and his own gun would supply him with food; and for the rest, he would spend his time in the study of the Bible, and seek for more light and direction from God.

"Such," continued the hermit, "is a slight sketch of the history of my country and of myself."

"Yourself!" exclaimed Martin.

"Yes. I am the Padre Caramuru; or rather, I *was*. I am padre no longer, but Senhor Carlos Caramuru, a merchant. Yet I know not what to do. When I look round upon my country and see how they know not the precious Word of God, my heart burns in me, and I sometimes think that it is my duty to go forth and preach."

"No doubt ye are right," said Barney. "I've always bin of opinion that when a man feels very strong in his heart on any partic'lar subject, it's a sure sign that the Almighty intends him to have something more to do with that subject than other men who don't feel about it at all."

The hermit remained silent for a few minutes. "I think you are right, friend," he said; "but I am very ignorant yet. I have no one to explain difficulties to me; and I fear to go about preaching lest I should preach what is not true. I will study yet for a time, and pray. After that, perhaps, I may go forth."

"But you have told us nothing yet about the trade of the country," said Martin, "or its size, or anything of that sort."

"I will soon tell you of that when I have lighted another cigar. This one does not draw well. Have you got a full pipe still, my friend?"

"All right, Mr. Carrymooroo," replied Barney,

knocking out the ashes. "I'll jist load wance more, and then—fire away."

In a few minutes the big cigar and short pipe were in full play, and the hermit continued:—

"This country is very large and very rich, but it is not well worked. The people are lazy, many of them, and have not much enterprise. Much is done, no doubt, but very much more *might* be done.

"The empire of Brazil occupies nearly one-half of the whole continent of South America. It is 2,600 miles long, and 2,500 miles broad, which, as you know perhaps, is a little larger than all Europe. The surface of the country is beautiful and varied. The hilly regions are very wild, although none of the mountains are very high, and the woods are magnificent; but a great part of the land consists of vast grassy plains, which are called llanos, or campos, or silvas. The campos along the banks of the River Amazon are equal to six times the size of France; and there is one great plain, lying between the Sierra Ibiapaba and the River Tocantins, which is 600 miles long by 400 miles broad. There are very few lakes in Brazil, and only one worth speaking of —the Lagoa dos Platos—which is 150 miles long. But our rivers are the finest in the whole world, being so long and wide and deep and free from falls that they afford splendid communication with the interior of the land. But, alas! there are few ships on these rivers yet, very few. The rivers in the north part of Brazil are so numerous and interlaced that they are much like the veins in the human body; and the great River Amazon and a few of its chief tributaries resemble the arteries.

"Then as to our produce," continued the hermit, "who can tell it all? We export sugar and coffee, and gold, silver, lead, zinc, quicksilver, and amethysts, and we have diamond mines—"

"Di'mond mines!" echoed Barney; "och, but I would like for to see them. Sure they would sparkle most beautiful. Are they far off, Mr. Carrymooroo?"

"Yes, very far off. Then we export dye-woods and cabinet-woods, and drugs, and gums, and hides—a great many hides, for the campos are full of wild cattle, and men hunt them on horseback, and catch them with a long rope called the *lasso*."

"How I should like to have a gallop over these great plains," murmured Martin.

"Then we have," continued the hermit, "rice, tapioca, cocoa, maize, wheat, mandioca, beans, bananas, pepper, cinnamon, oranges, figs, ginger, pine-apples, yams, lemons, mangoes, and many other fruits and vegetables. The mandioca you have eaten in the shape of farina. It is very good food; one acre gives as much nutriment as six acres of wheat.

"Of the trees you have seen something. There are thousands of kinds, and most magnificent. Some of them are more than thirty feet round about. There are two hundred different kinds of palms; and so thick stand the giant trees in many places, with creeping plants growing between, that it is not possible for man to cut his way through the forests in some parts. Language cannot describe the grandeur and glory of the Brazilian forests.

"We have numbers of wild horses, and hogs, and goats; and in the woods are tiger-cats, jaguars, tapirs, hyenas, sloths, porcupines, and—but you have seen many things already. If you live you will see more. I need not tell you of these things; very soon I will show you some.

"The population of my country consists of the descendants of Portuguese settlers, native Indians, and Negroes. Of the latter, some are free, some slaves. The Indians go about nearly naked. Most of them are in a savage state: they paint their skins, and wear gaudy ornaments. The religion of the country is Roman Catholic, but all religions are tolerated; and I have much hope for the future of Brazil, in spite of the priests."

"And do ye git much out o' the di'mond mines?" inquired Barney, whose mind was running on this subject.

"Oh yes, a great deal. Every year many are got, and Government gets one-fifth of the value of all the gold and diamonds found in the country. One diamond was found a short time ago which was worth £40,000."

"Ye don't say so!" exclaimed Barney in great surprise, as he blew an immense cloud of smoke from his lips. "Now, that's extr'or'nary. Why don't everybody go to the mines and dig up their fortin at wance?"

"Because men cannot *eat* diamonds," replied the hermit gravely.

"Troth, I niver thought o' that; ye're right."

Martin laughed heartily as he lay in his hammock and watched his friend's expression while pondering this weighty subject.

"Moreover," resumed the hermit, "you will be surprised to hear that diamond and gold finding is not the most profitable employment in the country.

"The man who cultivates the ground is better off than anybody. It is a fact, a very great fact, a fact that you should get firmly fixed in your memory—that in less than *two years* the exports of sugar and coffee amounted to more than the value of all the diamonds found in *eighty* years. Yes, that is true. But the people of Brazil are not well off. They have everything that is necessary to make a great nation; but we are not a great nation, far from it."

The hermit sighed deeply as he ceased speaking, and fell into an abstracted frame of mind.

"It's a great country intirely," said Barney, knocking the ashes out of his pipe, and placing that much-loved implement carefully in his pocket—"a great country; but there's a tremendous big screw loose somewhere."

"It seems curious to me," said Martin, in a ruminating tone of voice, "that people should not get on better in a country in which there is everything that man can desire to make him rich and happy. I wonder what it wants. Perhaps it's too hot, and the people want energy of character."

"Want energy!" shouted the hermit, leaping from his seat, and regarding his guests for a few moments with a stern expression of countenance; then, stretching forth his hand, he continued, in an excited tone: "Brazil does not want energy; it has only one want—it wants the Bible! When a country is sunk down in superstition and ignorance and moral depravity, so that the people know not right from wrong, there is only one cure for her—the Bible. Religion here is a mockery and a shame; such as, if it were better known, would make the heathen laugh in scorn. The priests are a curse to the land, not a blessing. Perhaps they are better in other lands—I know not; but well I know they are many of them false and wicked here. No truth is taught to the people—no Bible is read in their ears; religion is not taught— even morality is not taught; men follow the devices and desires of their own hearts, and there is no voice raised to say, 'You are doing wrong.' My country is sunk very low, and she cannot hope to rise, for the word of her Maker is not in her hand. True, there are a few, a very few Bibles in the great cities; but that is all—that cannot save her hundreds of towns and villages. Thousands of her people are slaves in body—all, all are slaves in soul; and yet you ask me what she wants. Ha! she wants *truth*—she wants to be purged of falsehood. She has bones and muscles, and arteries and veins—everything to make a strong and healthy nation; but she wants blood—she has no vital stream; yes, Brazil, my country, wants the Bible!"

CHAPTER XII.

A hunting expedition, in which are seen stones that can run, and cows that require no food—Besides a desperate encounter with a jaguar, and other strange things.

FOR many weeks Martin Rattler and his friend Barney O'Flannagan continued to dwell with the hermit in his forest home, enjoying his entertaining and instructive discourse, and joining with him in the hunting expeditions which he undertook for the purpose of procuring fresh food for his table. In these rambles they made constant discoveries of something new and surprising, in reference to both the vegetables and animals of that extraordinary region of the earth. They also had many adventures—some amusing and some terrible—which we cannot enlarge on here, for they would fill ten volumes such as this were they to be all recorded in detail.

One day the hermit roused them earlier than usual and told them to get ready, as he intended to go a considerable distance that day, and he wished to reach a particular spot before the heat of noon. So Martin and Barney despatched breakfast in as short a time as possible, and the hermit read them a chapter out of his large and well-thumbed Bible, after which they equipped themselves for the chase.

When Martin and his friend escaped from the pirates and landed on the coast of Brazil, they were clothed in sailor-like costume, namely, white duck trousers, coloured flannel shirts, blue jackets, round straw hats, and strong shoes. This costume was not very suitable for the warm climate in which they now found themselves, so their hospitable friend the hermit gave them two loose light cotton coats or jackets, of a blue colour, and broad brimmed straw hats similar to his own. He also gave them two curious garments called *ponchos*. The poncho serves the purpose of cloak and blanket. It is simply a square dark-coloured blanket with a hole in the middle of it, through which the head is thrust in rainy weather, and the garment hangs down all round. At night the poncho is useful as a covering. The hermit wore a loose open hunting-coat, and underneath it a girdle, in which was a long sharp knife and a brace of pistols. His trousers were of blue-striped cotton. He usually carried a double-barrelled gun over his shoulder, and a powder-horn and bullet-bag were slung round his neck. Barney now procured from this hospitable man a supply of powder and shot for his large brass-mounted cavalry pistol. The hermit also made him a present of a long hunting-knife; and he gave one of a smaller size to Martin. As Martin had no weapon, the hermit manufactured for him a stout bow and quiver full of arrows, with which, after some practice, he became reasonably expert.

Thus armed, they sallied forth, and following the footpath that conducted from the door of the hut to the brow of the hill opposite, they were soon buried in the shades of the great forest. On this particular morning, Barney observed that the hermit carried with him a stout spear, which he was not usually in the habit of doing. Being of an inquisitive disposition, he inquired the reason of his taking it.

"I expect to find a jaguar to-day," answered the hermit. "I saw him yesterday go down into the small valley in which my cows grow. I will show you my cows soon, Martin."

The hermit stopped short suddenly as he spoke, and pointed to a large bird, about fifty yards in advance of them. It seemed to bear a particular ill-will to a round rough stone which it pecked most energetically. After a few minutes the bird ceased its attacks and flew off; whereupon the rough stone opened itself out, and, running quickly away, burrowed into a little hole and disappeared!

"That is an armadillo," remarked the hermit, continuing to lead the way through the woods. "It is covered with a coat of mail, as you see; and when enemies come it rolls itself up like a ball and lies like a hard stone till they go away. But it has four little legs, and with them it burrows so quickly that we cannot dig it up, and must smoke it out of its hole—which I do often, because it is very good to eat, as you very well know."

While they continued thus to walk through the woods conversing, Martin and Barney were again interested and amused by the immense number of brilliant parrots and toucans which swooped about, chattering from tree to tree, in large flocks. Sometimes thirty or forty of the latter would come screaming through the woods and settle upon the dark-green foliage of a coffee-tree; the effect of which was to give the tree the appearance of having been suddenly loaded with ripe golden fruit. Then the birds would catch sight of the travellers and fly screaming away, leaving the tree dark-green and fruitless as before. The little green parrots were the most outrageously noisy things that ever lived. Not content with screaming when they flew, they continued to shriek, apparently with delight, while they devoured the seeds of the gorgeous sun-flowers; and more than once Martin was prompted to scatter a handful of stones among them, as a hint to be less noisy; but this only made them worse—like a bad baby, which, the more you tell it to be quiet, sets to work the more earnestly to increase and add to the vigour of its roaring. So Martin wisely let the parrots alone. They also startled, in passing through swampy places, several large blue herons and long-legged cranes; and on many of the trees they observed the curious hanging nests of a bird, which the hermit told them was the large oriole. These nests hung in long strings from the tops of the palm-trees, and the birds were very actively employed moving about and chattering round their swinging villages; on seeing which Martin could not help remarking that it would astonish the colony not a little, if the top house were to give way and let all the mansions below come tumbling to the ground!

They were disappointed, however, in not seeing monkeys gambolling among the trees, as they had expected.

"Ah! my friends," said the hermit, "travellers in my country are very often disappointed. They come here expecting to see everything all at once; but although there are jaguars, and serpents, and bears, and monkeys, plenty of them, as your ears can tell you, these creatures keep out of the sight of man as much as possible. They won't come out of the woods and show themselves to please travellers. You have been very lucky since you arrived. Many travellers go about for months together and do not see half so much as you."

"That's thrue," observed Barney, with his head a little on one side, and his eyes cast up in a sort of meditative frown, as if he were engaged in subjecting the hermit's remarks to a process of severe philosophical contemplation; "but I would be very well plazed av the wild bastes would show themselves now and then, for—"

Martin Rattler burst into a loud laugh, for Barney's upward glance of contemplation was suddenly transformed into a gaze of intense astonishment, as he beheld the blue countenance of a large red monkey staring down upon him from amid the branches of an overhanging tree. The monkey's face expressed, if possible, greater surprise than that of the Irishman, and its mouth was partially open and thrust forward in a sort of threatening and inquiring manner. There seemed to be some bond of sympathy between the monkey and the man, for while *its* mouth opened *his* mouth opened too.

"A-a-a-a-a—ah!" exclaimed the monkey.

A facetious smile overspread Barney's face. "Och! be all manes; the same to you, kindly," said he, taking off his hat and making a low bow.

The civility did not seem to be appreciated, however; for the monkey put on a most indignant frown and displayed a terrific double row of long brilliant teeth and red gums, while it uttered a shriek of passion, twisted its long tail round a branch, and hurled itself, with a motion more like that of a bird than a beast, into the midst of the tree and disappeared, leaving Martin and Barney and the hermit each with a very broad grin on his countenance.

The hunters now arrived at an open space where there were several large umbrageous trees, and as it was approaching mid-day they resolved to rest here for a couple of hours. Birds and insects were gradually becoming more and more silent, and soon afterwards the only sounds that broke upon their ears were the curious metallic notes of the urupongas, or bell-birds, which were so like to the rapid beating of a smith's hammer on an anvil, that it was with the greatest difficulty Barney was restrained from going off by himself in search of the "smiddy." Indeed he began to suspect that the worthy hermit was deceiving him, and was only fully convinced at last when he saw one of the birds. It was pure white, about the size of a thrush, and had a curious horn or fleshy tubercle upon its head.

Having rested and refreshed themselves, they resumed their journey a short time before the noisy inhabitants of the woods recommenced their active afternoon operations.

"Hallo! what's that?" cried Barney, starting back and drawing his pistol, while Martin hastily fitted an arrow to his bow.

Not ten paces in front of them a frightful monster ran across their path, which seemed so hideous to Martin that his mind instantly reverted to the fable of St. George and the Dragon, and he almost expected to see fire issuing from its mouth. It was a huge lizard, with a body about three feet long, covered with bright scales. It had a long, thick tail. Its head was clumsy and misshapen, and altogether its aspect was very horrible. Before either Martin or Barney could fire, the hermit dropped his gun and spear, sprang quickly forward, caught the animal by the tail, and, putting forth his great strength to the utmost, swung it round his head and dashed its brains out against a tree.

Barney and Martin could only stare with amazement.

"This we call an iguana," said the hermit, as he piled a number of heavy stones on the carcass to preserve it from other animals. "It is very good to eat—as good as chicken. This is not a very big one; they are sometimes five feet long, but almost quite harmless—not venomous at all; and the only means he has to defend himself is the tail, which is very powerful, and gives a tremendously hard blow. But, as you see, if you catch him quickly he can do nothing."

"It's all very well for you, or even Barney here, to talk of catching him by the tail," said Martin, smiling; "but it would have puzzled me to swing that fellow round my head."

"Arrah! ye're right, boy; I doubt if I could have done it mesilf," said Barney.

"No fear," said the hermit, patting Martin's broad shoulders as he passed him and led the way; "you will be strong enough for that very soon—as strong as me in a year or two."

They now proceeded down into a somewhat dark and closely wooded valley, through which meandered a small rivulet. Here they had some difficulty in forcing their way through the dense underwood and broad leaves, most of which seemed very strange to Martin and his comrade, being so gigantic. There were also many kinds of ferns, which sometimes arched over their heads and completely shut out the view, while some of them crept up the trees like climbing-plants. Emerging from this, they came upon a more open space, in the midst of which grew a number of majestic trees.

"There are my cows!" said the hermit, pausing as he spoke, and pointing towards a group of tall straight-stemmed trees that were the noblest in appearance they had yet seen. "Good cows they are," he continued, going up to one and making a notch in the bark with his axe; "they need no feeding or looking after, yet, as you see, they are always ready to give me cream."

While he spoke, a thick white liquid flowed from the notch in the bark into a cocoa-nut drinking-cup, which the hermit always carried at his girdle. In a few minutes he presented his visitors with a draught of what they declared was most excellent cream.

The masseranduba, or milk-tree, as it is called, is indeed one of the most wonderful of all the extraordinary trees in the forests of Brazil, and is one among many instances of the bountiful manner in which God provides for the wants of his creatures. No doubt this might with equal truth be said of all the gifts that a beneficent Creator bestows upon mankind; but when, as in the case of this milk-tree, the provision for our wants comes in a singular and striking manner, it seems fitting and appropriate that we should specially acknowledge the gift as coming from the hand of Him who giveth us all things liberally to enjoy.

The milk-tree rises with a straight stem to an enormous height, and the fruit, about the size of a small apple, is full of rich and juicy pulp, and is very good. The timber, also, is hard, fine-grained, and durable—particularly adapted for such works as are exposed to the weather. But its most remarkable peculiarity is the rich vegetable milk which flows in abundance from it when the bark is cut. This milk is so like to that of the cow in taste, that it can scarcely be distinguished from it, having only a very slight peculiarity of flavour, which is rather agreeable than otherwise. In tea and coffee it has the same effect as rich cream, and, indeed, is so thick that it requires to be diluted with water before being used. This milk is also employed as glue. It hardens when exposed to the air, and becomes very tough and slightly elastic, and is said to be quite as good and useful as ordinary glue.

Having partaken of as much milk as they desired, they continued their journey a little further, when they came to a spur of the sierra, or mountain range, that cuts through that part of the country. Here the ground became more rugged, but still densely covered with wood, and rocks lay piled about in many places, forming several dark and gloomy caverns. The hermit now unslung his gun and advanced to the foot of a cliff, near the farther end of which there were several caves, the mouths of which were partially closed with long ferns and masses of luxuriant vegetation.

"Now we must be prepared," said the hermit, feeling the point of his spear. "I think there is a jaguar here. I saw him yesterday, and I am quite sure he will not go away till he tries to do some mischief. He little knows that there is nothing here to hurt but me."

The hermit chuckled as he said this, and resting his gun against the cliff near the entrance to the first cave, which was a small one, he passed on to the next. Holding the spear in his left hand, he threw a stone violently into the cavern. Barney and Martin listened and gazed in silent expectation; but they only heard the hollow sound of the falling stone as it dashed against the sides of the cave, then all was still.

"Och, then, he's off," cried Barney.

"Hush," said Martin; "don't speak till he has tried the other cave."

Without taking notice of their remarks, the hermit repeated the experiment at the mouths of two caverns farther on, with the like result.

"Maybe the spalpeen's hidin' in the little cave where ye laid down yer gun," suggested Barney, going towards the place as he spoke. "Och, then, come here, friend; sure it must be the mouth of a mine, for there's two o' the beautifullest di'monds I iver—"

Barney's speech was cut short by a low peculiar sound, that seemed like the muttering of far-distant thunder. At the same moment the hermit pulled him violently back, and placing himself in a firm attitude full in front of the cavern, held the point of the spear advanced before him.

"Martin," he whispered, "shoot an arrow straight into that hole—quick!"

Martin obeyed, and the arrow whizzed through the aperture. Instantly there issued from it a savage and tremendous roar, so awful that it seemed as if the very mountain were bellowing and that the cavern were its mouth. But not a muscle of the hermit's figure moved. He stood like a bronze statue, his head thrown back and his chest advanced, with one foot planted firmly before him and the spear pointing towards the cave. It seemed strange to Martin that a man should face what appeared to him unknown danger so boldly and calmly; but he did not consider that the hermit knew exactly the amount of danger before him. He knew precisely the manner in which it would assail him, and he knew just what was necessary to be done in order to avert it; and in the strength of that knowledge he stood unmoved, with a slight smile upon his tightly-compressed lips.

Scarcely had the roar ceased when it was repeated with tenfold fierceness; the bushes and fern leaves shook violently, and an enormous and beautifully-spotted jaguar shot through the air as if it had been discharged from a cannon's mouth. The hermit's eye wavered not; he bent forward a hair's-breadth; the glittering spear-point touched the animal's breast, pierced through it, and came out at its side below the ribs. But the force of the bound was too great for the strength of the weapon: the handle snapped in twain, and the transfixed jaguar struck down the hermit and fell writhing upon him!

In the excitement of the moment Barney drew his pistol from his belt and snapped it at the animal. It was well for the hermit at that moment that Barney had forgotten to prime his weapon; for although he aimed at the jaguar's skull, there is no doubt whatever that he would have blown out the hermit's brains. Before he could make a second attempt, Martin sprang towards the gun which leaned against the cliff, and running quickly up, he placed the muzzle close to the jaguar's ear and lodged a bullet in its brain. All this was done in a few seconds, and the hermit regained his legs just as the animal fell dead. Fortunately he was not hurt, having adroitly avoided the sharp claws of his enemy.

"Arrah! Mister Hermit," said Barney, wiping the perspiration from his forehead, "it's yersilf that was well-nigh done for this time, an' no mistake. Did iver I see sich a spring! an' ye stud the charge jist like a stone wall—niver moved a fut!"

"Are you not hurt?" inquired Martin, somewhat anxiously; "your face is all covered with blood."

"Yes, boy, but it is the blood of the jaguar; thanks to you for your quick hand, I am not hurt at all."

The hermit washed his face in the neighbouring brook, and then proceeded to skin the jaguar, the carcass being worthless. After which they retraced their steps through the woods as quickly as possible, for the day was now far spent, and the twilight, as we have before remarked, is so short in tropical latitudes that travellers require to make sure of reaching the end of the day's journey towards evening, unless they choose to risk losing their way, and spending the night in the forest.

They picked up the iguana in passing; and on reaching the spot where the armadillo had burrowed, the hermit paused and kindled a small fire over the hole, by means of his flint, steel, and tinder-box. He thus contrived to render the creature's habitation so uncomfortable that it rushed hurriedly out; then, observing that its enemies were waiting, it doubled its head and tail together, and became the image of a rough stone.

"Poor thing," said Martin, as the hermit killed it, "that reminds me of the ostrich of the desert, which, I'm told, when it is chased over the plains by men on horseback, and finds that it cannot escape, thrusts its head into a bush, and fancies, no doubt, that it cannot be seen, although its great body is visible a mile off!"

"Martin," said Barney, "this arth is full o' quare craturs intirely."

"That's true, Barney; and not the least 'quare' among them is an Irishman, a particular friend of mine!"

"Hould yer tongue, ye spalpeen, or I'll put yer head in the wather!"

"I wish ye would, Barney, for it is terribly hot

and mosquito-bitten, and you couldn't have suggested anything more delightful. But here we are once more at our forest home; and now for a magnificent cup of coffee and a mandioca-cake."

"Not to mintion," added Barney, "a juicy steak of Igu Anny, an' a tender chop o' Army Dillo."

CHAPTER XIII.

Martin and Barney continue their travels, and see strange things—Among others, they see living jewels—They go to see a festa—They fight and run away.

MARTIN RATTLER and Barney O'Flannagan soon after this began to entertain a desire to travel farther into the interior of Brazil, and behold with their own eyes the wonders of which they had heard so much from their kind and hospitable friend the hermit. Martin was specially anxious to see the great river Amazon, about which he entertained the most romantic ideas—as well he might, for there is not such another river in the world for size, and for the many curious things connected with its waters and its banks. Barney, too, was smitten with an intense desire to visit the diamond mines, which he fancied must be the most brilliant and beautiful sight in the whole world; and when Martin asked him what sort of place he expected to see, he used to say that he "pictur'd in his mind a great many deep and lofty caverns, windin' in an' out an' round about, with the sides and the floors and the ceilin's all of a blaze with glittering di'monds, an' top'zes, an' purls, an' what not; with Naiggurs be the dozen picking them up in handfuls. An' sure," he would add, "if we was wance there, we could fill our pockets in no time, an' then, hooray for ould Ireland! an' live like imperors for ivermore."

"But you forget, Barney, the account the hermit has given us of the mines. He evidently does not think that much is to be made of them."

"Och! niver mind the hermit. There's always good luck attends Barney O'Flannagan. An' sure if nobody wint for fear they would git nothing, all the di'monds that iver came out o' the mines would be lyin' there still. An' didn't he tell us there was wan got only a short time since, worth I don't know how many thousand pounds? Arrah! if I don't go to the mines an' git one the size o' me head, I'll let ye rig me out with a long tail an' set me adrift in the woods for a blue-faced monkey."

It so happened that this was the time when the hermit was in the habit of setting out on one of his trading-trips; and when Martin told him of the desire that he and Barney entertained to visit the interior, he told them that he would be happy to take them along with him, provided they would act the part of muleteers. To this they readily agreed, being only too glad of an opportunity of making some return to their friend, who refused to accept any payment for his hospitality, although Barney earnestly begged of him to accept of his watch, which was the only object of value he was possessed of—and that wasn't worth much, being made of pinchbeck, and utterly incapable of going! Moreover, he relieved their minds by telling them that they would easily obtain employment as canoemen on the Amazon, for men were very difficult to be got on that river to man the boats; and if they could stand the heat, and were willing to work like Indians, they might travel as far as they pleased. To which Martin replied, in his ignorance, that he thought he could stand anything; and Barney roundly asserted that, having been burnt to a cinder long ago in the "East Injies," it was impossible to overdo him any more.

Under these circumstances, therefore, they started three weeks later to visit a populous town about twenty miles off, from which they set out on their travels with a string of heavily-laden mules, crossed the low countries or campos lying near to the sea, and began to ascend the sierras that divide this portion of Brazil from the country which is watered by the innumerable rivers that flow into the mighty Amazon.

The cavalcade consisted of ten mules, each with two goodly-sized bales of merchandise on its back. They were driven and attended to by Negroes, whose costume consisted of a light cotton shirt with short sleeves, and a pair of loose cotton drawers reaching down to the knee. With the exception of a straw hat this was all they wore. Martin, and Barney, and the hermit each bestrode a mule, with a small bale slung on either side, over the front of which their legs dangled comfortably. They had ponchos with them, strapped to the mules' backs, and each carried a clumsy umbrella to shield him from the fierce rays of the sun; but our two adventurers soon became so hardened and used to the climate, that they dispensed with the umbrellas altogether.

The sierra or mountain range over which they passed was about thirty miles in extent, being in some places quite level and open, but in others somewhat rugged, and covered with large but thinly scattered trees, the most common of which had fine darkgreen glossy leaves, with spikes of bright yellow flowers terminating the branchlets. There were also many peculiar shrubs and flowering plants, of a sort that the travellers had never seen the like of in their native land.

"How I wish," said Martin with a sigh, as he rode

along beside his friend Barney, "that I knew something of botany."

Barney opened his eyes in surprise. "Arrah! it's too much of a philosopher ye are already, lad. What good would it do ye to know all the hard names that men have given to the flowers? Sure I wance wint after the doctor o' a ship, to carry his box for him when he wint on what he called botanical excursions; and the poor cratur used to be pokin' his nose for iver down at the ground, an' peerin' through his green spectacles at miserable bits o' plants, an' niver seemin' to enjoy anything; when all the time *I* was lookin' far fornint me an' all around me, an' up at the sky, seein' ivery beautiful thing, and snifterin' up the sweet smells, an' in fact enjoyin' the whole univarse —an' my pipe to boot—like an intelligent cratur."

Barney looked round as he spoke with a bland, self-satisfied expression of countenance, as if he felt that he had given a lucid definition of the very highest style of philosophy, and proved that he, Barney O'Flannagan, was possessed of the same in no common degree.

"Well, Barney," rejoined Martin, "since you give me credit for being a philosopher, I must continue to talk philosophically. Your botanical friend took a *microscopic* view of nature, while you took a *telescopic* view of it. Each view is good, but both views are better; and I can't help wishing that I were more of a philosopher than I am, especially in reference to botany."

"Humph!" ejaculated Barney, who seemed not quite to understand his young friend, "yer observations are remarkably thrue, and do ye great credit, for yer years.—Ah! Mr. Hermit, good luck to ye! I'm glad to see that ye've got some consideration for man and baste. I'm quite ready for my victuals, and so's my mule;—aren't you, avic?"

Barney's latter remark was addressed to his patient charger, from whose back he sprang as he spoke, and slackened its girths.

It was now approaching mid-day, and the hermit had pitched upon a large tree as a fitting spot for rest and refreshment. Water had been brought up the mountain in a huge calabash; but they did not require to use it, as they found a quantity in the hollow stump of a tree. There were several frogs swimming about in this miniature lake; but it was found to be fresh and clear and good notwithstanding.

Towards evening they passed a string of mules going towards the town which they had just left. They were driven by Negroes, most of whom were slaves, and nearly quite naked. A Brazilian merchant, wearing a picturesque broad-brimmed, high-crowned straw-hat, a poncho, and brown leather boots armed at the heels with large sharp spurs, rode at the head, and gave the strangers a surly nod of his head as they passed. Soon after, they descended into the plain, and came to a halt at a sort of road-side public-house, where there was no sleeping accommodation, but where they found an open shed in which travellers placed their goods, and slung their hammocks, and attended to themselves. At the venda, close beside it, they purchased a large bag of farina, being short of that necessary article of food, and then set to work to prepare supper in the open air; while the merry Negroes, who seemed to enjoy life most thoroughly, laughed and sang as they removed the bales from the mules' backs and cooked their simple fare.

Barney's cooking propensities now came into full play, and with the variety of fruits and vegetables which the country afforded he exercised his ingenuity, and produced several dishes of so savoury a nature that the hermit was compelled to open his eyes in amazement and smack his lips with satisfaction, being quite unable to express his sentiments in words. While thus busily and agreeably employed, they were told by the owner of the venda that a *festa* was being celebrated at a village about a league distant from where they stood.

"I should like to see it above all things," said Martin eagerly; "could we not go?"

The hermit frowned. "Yes, we can go, but it will be to behold folly. Perhaps it will be a good lesson from which much may be learned. We will go."

"It's not a step that I'll budge till I've finished me pipe," said Barney, pulling away at that bosom friend with unexampled energy. "To smoke," he continued, winking gently with one eye, "is the first law of nature; jist give me ten minutes more, an' I'm your man for anything."

Being a fine evening, they proceeded on foot. In about an hour after setting out they approached the village, which lay in a beautiful valley below them. Sounds of mirth and music rose like a distant murmur on the air, and mingled with the songs of birds and insects. Then the sun went down, and in a few minutes it grew dark, while the brilliant fire-flies began their nocturnal gambols. Suddenly a bright flame burst over the village, and a flight of magnificent rockets shot up into the sky, and burst in a hundred bright and variously-coloured stars, which paled for a few seconds the lights of nature. But they vanished in a moment, and the clear stars shed abroad their undying lustre, seeming, in their quiet, unfading beauty, a gentle satire on the short-lived and gairish productions of man.

"Mighty purty, no doubt," exclaimed Barney. "Is this the Imperor's birth-day?"

"No," replied the hermit, shaking his head; "that is the way in which the false priests amuse the people. The poor Indian and the Negro, and, indeed, the ignorant Brazilian, thinks it very grand; and the priests let them think it is pleasing to the God of heaven. Ah! here comes an old Negro; we will ask him."

Several country people, in varied and picturesque costumes, hurried past the travellers towards the village; and as they came to a foot-path that joined the road, an old Negro approached them. Saluting him in the Portuguese language, the hermit said, "Friend, why do they let off rockets to-night?"

"Por Dios" (for God), answered the old man, looking and pointing upwards with grave solemnity. Without vouchsafing another word, he hurried away.

"So they think," said the hermit, "and so they are taught by the priests. Music, noise, and fire-works please these ignorant people; and so the priests, who are mostly as ignorant as the people, tell them it is a good part of religious ceremony."

Presently a band of young girls came laughing and

singing along the road. They were dressed in pure white, their rich black tresses being uncovered and ornamented with flowers and what appeared to be bright jewels.

"Hallo!" exclaimed Martin, gazing after them; "what splendid jewels! Surely these must be the daughters of very rich people."

"Och, but they've been at the di'mond mines for certain! Did iver ye sae the like?"

The girls did indeed seem to blaze with jewels, which not only sparkled in their hair, but fringed their white robes, and were worked round the edges of their slippers; so that a positive light shone around their persons, and fell upon the path like a halo, giving them more the appearance of lovely supernatural beings than the daughters of earth.

"These jewels," said the hermit, "were never polished by the hands of men. They are fire-flies."

"Fire-flies!" exclaimed Martin and Barney simultaneously.

"Yes, they are living fire-flies. The girls very often catch them and tie them up in little bits of gauze, and put them, as you see, on their dresses and in their hair. To my mind they seem more beautiful far than diamonds. Sometimes the Indians, when they travel at night, fix fire-flies to their feet, and so have good lamps to their path."

While Barney was expressing his surprise at this information in very racy language, they entered the village, and mingling with the throng of holiday-keepers, followed the stream towards the grand square.

The church, which seemed to be a centre of attraction, and was brilliantly illuminated, was a neat wooden building with two towers. The streets of the village were broad and straggling; and so luxuriant was the vegetation, and so lazy the nature of the inhabitants, that it seemed as if the whole place were overgrown with gigantic weeds. Shrubs and creeping-plants grew in the neglected gardens, climbed over the palings, and straggled about the streets. Plants grew on the tops of the houses, ferns peeped out under the eaves; and, in short, on looking at it, one had the feeling that ere long the whole place, people and all, must be smothered in superabundant vegetation!

The houses were all painted white or yellow, with the doors and windows bright green—just like grown-up toys; and sounds of revelry, with now and then the noise of disputation, issued from many of them.

It is impossible to describe minutely the appearance

of the motley crowd through which our adventurers elbowed their way, gazing curiously on the strange scene, which seemed to them more like a dream than a reality, after their long sojourn in the solitudes of the forest. Processions headed by long-robed priests with flambeaux and crucifixes; young girls in light costumes and long white cotton shawls, selling sweet cakes of mandioca flour and bonbons; swarthy Brazilians, some in white jackets, loose cotton drawers, and straw hats, others in brown leather boots and ponchos; Negroes in short white drawers and shirts, besides many without any clothing above their waists; Indians from the interior, copper-coloured, and some of them, fine-looking men, having only a strip of cloth about their loins;—such were the strange crew whose loud voices, added to the whiz of rockets, squibs, crackers, guns, and musical instruments, created a deafening noise.

In the midst of the village there was a tree of such enormous size that it quite took our travellers by surprise. It was a wild fig-tree, capable of sheltering a thousand persons under its shadow! Here a spirited *fandango* was going on, and they stood for some time watching the movements of the performers. Growing tired of this, they wandered about until they came to a less crowded part of the village, and entered a pleasant grove of trees skirting the road by which they had arrived. While sauntering here, enjoying the cool night breeze and delicious perfume of flowers, a woman uttered a piercing shriek near to them. It was instantly followed by loud voices in altercation. Ever ready to fly to the help of womankind, and, generally, to assist in a " row," Barney darted through the bushes, and came upon the scene of action just in time to see the white skirt of a female's dress disappear down an avenue, and to behold two Brazilians savagely writhing in mortal strife. At the moment he came up, one of the combatants had overcome the other, and a fierce smile of triumph crossed his swarthy countenance as he raised his gleaming knife.

" Och, ye murtherer! would ye attimpt that same?" cried Barney, catching the man by the wrist and hurling him on his back. The other sprang up on being thus unexpectedly freed, and darted away; while the thwarted man uttered a yell of disappointment, and sprang like a tiger at Barney's throat. A blow, however, from the Irishman's fist, quietly delivered, and straight between the eyes, stretched the Brazilian on the ground. At the same moment a party of men, attracted by the cries, burst through the bushes and surrounded the successful champion. Seeing their countryman apparently dead upon the ground, they rushed upon Barney in a body; but the first who came within reach was floored in an instant, and the others were checked in their career by the sudden appearance of the hermit and Martin Rattler. The noise of many voices, as of people hastening towards them, was heard at the same time.

"We have no time to lose; do as I bid you," whispered the hermit. Whirling a heavy stick round his head the hermit shouted the single word "Charge!" and dashed forward.

Barney and Martin obeyed. Three Brazilians went down like ninepins; the rest turned and fled precipitately.

"Now, run for life!" cried the hermit, setting the example. Barney hesitated to follow what he deemed a cowardly flight, but the yells of the natives returning in strong force decided the question. He and Martin took to their heels with right good will, and in a few minutes the three friends were far on the road which led to their night bivouac; while the villagers, finding pursuit hopeless, returned to the village, and continued the wild orgies of their festa.

CHAPTER XIV.

Cogitations and canoeing on the Amazon—Barney's exploit with an alligator—Stubborn facts—Remarkable mode of sleeping.

IT is pleasant, when the sun is bright, and the trees are green, and when flowering shrubs and sweet-smelling tropical trees scent the balmy atmosphere at eventide, to lie extended at full length in a canoe, and drop easily, silently, yet quickly down the current of a noble river, under the grateful shadow of overhanging foliage; and to look lazily up at the bright blue sky which appears in broken patches among the verdant leaves, or down at the river in which that bright sky and those green leaves are reflected, or aside at the mud-banks where greedy vultures are searching for prey and lazy alligators are basking in the sun; and to listen, the while, to the innumerable cries and notes of monkeys, toucans, parrots, orioles, bemtevi or fly-catchers, white-winged and blue chatterers, and all the myriads of birds and beasts that cause the forests of Brazil, above all other forests in the world probably, to resound with the gleeful songs of animated nature!

It is pleasant to be thus situated, especially when a cool breeze blows the mosquitoes and other insects off the water, and relieves you for a time from their incessant attacks. Martin Rattler found it pleasant, as he thus lay on his back with his diminutive pet marmoset monkey seated on his breast quietly picking the kernel out of a nut. And Barney O'Flannagan found it pleasant, as he lay extended in the bow of the canoe with his head leaning over the edge, gazing abstractedly at his own reflected visage, while his hands trailed through the cool water, and his young dog—a shaggy, indescribable beast with a bluff nose and a bushy tail—watched him intently, as a mother might watch an only child in a dangerous situation. And the old, sun-dried, and storm-battered, and time-shrivelled mulatto trader, in whose canoe they were embarked, and whose servants they had become, found it pleasant, as he sat there perched in his little *montaria*, like an exceedingly ancient and overgrown monkey, guiding it safely down the waters of the great river of the Tocantins.

Some months have passed since we last parted from our daring adventurers. During that period they had crossed an immense tract of country, and reached the head-waters of one of the many streams that carry the surplus moisture of central Brazil into the Amazon.

Here they found an old trader, a free mulatto, whose crew of Indians had deserted him—a common thing in that country—and who gladly accepted their services, agreeing to pay them a small wage. And here they sorrowfully, and with many expressions of good-will, parted from their kind friend and entertainer the hermit. His last gift to Martin was the wonderfully small marmoset monkey before mentioned; and his parting souvenir to Barney was the bluff-nosed dog that watched over him with maternal care, and loved him next to itself;—as well it might, for if everybody had been of the same spirit as Barney O'Flannagan, the Act for the Prevention of Cruelty to Animals would never have been passed in Britain.

It was a peculiar and remarkable and altogether extraordinary monkey, that tiny marmoset. There was a sort of romance connected with it, too; for it had been the mother of an indescribably small infant-monkey, which was killed at the time of its mother's capture. It drank coffee, too, like—like a Frenchman, and would by no means retire to rest at night until it had had its usual allowance. Then it would fold its delicate little hands on its bosom, and close its eyes with an expression of solemn grief, as if, having had its last earthly wish gratified, it now resigned itself to—sleep. Martin loved it deeply, but his love was unrequited; for, strange to say, that small monkey lavished all its affection on Barney's shaggy dog. And the dog knew it, and was evidently proud of it, and made no objection whatever to the monkey sitting on his back, or his head, or his nose, or doing, in fact, whatever it chose whenever it pleased. When in the canoe, the marmoset played with Grampus, as the dog was named; and when on shore, it invariably travelled on his back.

Martin used to lie in the canoe half asleep and watch the little face of the marmoset, until, by some unaccountable mental process, he came to think of Aunt Dorothy Grumbit. Often did poor Martin dream of his dear old aunt, while sleeping under the shelter of these strange-leaved tropical trees and surrounded by the wild sounds of that distant land, until he dreamed himself back again in the old village. Then he would rush to the well-known school, and find all the boys there except Bob Croaker, who he felt certain must be away drowning the white kitten; and off he would go and catch him, sure enough, in the very act, and would give him the old thrashing over again, with all the additional vigour acquired during his rambles abroad thrown into it. Then he would run home in eager haste, and find old Mrs.

Grumbit hard at the one thousand nine hundred and ninety-ninth pair of worsted socks; and fat Mr. Arthur Jollyboy sitting opposite to her, dressed in the old lady's bed-curtain chintz and high-crowned cap, with the white kitten in his arms and his spectacles on his chin, watching the process with intense interest, and cautioning her not to forget the "hitch" by any means; whereupon the kitten would fly up in his face, and Mr. Jollyboy would dash through the window with a loud howl, and Mrs. Grumbit's face would turn blue, and, uncoiling an enormous tail, she would bound shrieking after him in among the trees and disappear! Martin usually wakened at this point, and found the marmoset gazing in his face with an expression of sorrowful solemnity, and the old sun-dried trader staring vacantly before him as he steered his light craft down the broad stream of the Tocantins.

The trader could speak little more English than sufficed to enable him to say "yes" and "no;" Barney could speak about as much Portuguese as enabled him to say "no" and "yes;" while Martin, by means of a slight smattering of that language, which he had picked up by ear during the last few months, mixed now and then with a word or two of Latin, and helped out by a clever use of the language of signs, succeeded in becoming the link of communication between the two.

For many weeks they continued to descend the river; paddling energetically when the stream was sluggish, and resting comfortably when the stream was strong, and sometimes dragging their canoe over rocks and sand-banks to avoid rapids—passing many villages and plantations of the natives by the way—till at last they swept out upon the bosom of the great Amazon river.

The very first thing they saw upon entering it was an enormous alligator, fully eighteen feet long, sound asleep on a mud-bank.

"Och! put ashore, ye Naygur," cried Barney, seizing his pistol and rising up in the bow of the canoe. The old man complied quickly, for his spirit was high and easily roused.

"Look out now, Martin, an' hould back the dog for fear he wakes him up," said Barney, in a hoarse whisper, as he stepped ashore and hastened stealthily towards the sleeping monster, catching up a handful of gravel as he went and ramming it down the barrel of his pistol. It was a wonderful pistol that—an Irish one by birth, and absolutely incapable of bursting, else assuredly it would have gone, as its owner said, to "smithereens" long ago.

Barney was not a good stalker. The alligator awoke, and made for the water as fast as it could waddle. The Irishman rushed forward close up, as it plunged into the river, and discharged the compound of lead and stones right against the back of its head. He might as well have fired at the boiler of a steam-engine. The entire body of an alligator—back and belly, head and tail—is so completely covered with thick hard scales, that shot has no effect on it; and even a bullet cannot pierce its coat of mail, except in one or two vulnerable places. Nevertheless the shot had been fired so close to it that the animal was stunned, and rolled over on its back in the water. Seeing this, the old trader rushed in up to his chin and caught it by the tail; but at the same moment the monster recovered, and, turning round, displayed its terrific rows of teeth. The old man uttered a dreadful roar, and struggled to the land as fast as he could; while the alligator, equally frightened, no doubt, gave a magnificent flourish and splash with its tail, and dived to the bottom of the river.

The travellers returned disgusted to their canoe, and resumed their journey up the Amazon in silence.

The vulnerable places about an alligator are the soft parts under the throat and the joints of the legs.

This is well known to the jaguar, its mortal foe, which attacks it on land, and fastening on these soft parts, soon succeeds in killing it; but should the alligator get the jaguar into its powerful jaws, or catch it in the water, it is certain to come off the conqueror.

The Amazon, at its mouth, is more like a wide lake or arm of the sea than a river. Mention has been already made of this noble stream in the hermit's story; but it is worthy of more particular notice, for truly the Amazon is in many respects a wonderful river. It is the largest, though not quite the longest, in the world. Taking its rise among the rocky solitudes of the great mountain range of the Andes, it flows through nearly four thousand miles of the continent in an easterly direction, trending northward towards its mouth, and entering the Atlantic Ocean on the northern coast of South America, directly under the equator. In its course it receives the waters of nearly all the great rivers of central South America, and thousands of smaller tributaries, so that when it reaches the ocean its volume of water is enormous. Some idea may be formed of its majestic size from the fact that one of its tributaries—the Rio Negro—is fifteen hundred miles long, and varying in breadth, being a mile wide not far from its mouth, while higher up it spreads out in some places into sheets of ten miles in width. The Madeira, another tributary, is also a river of the largest size. The Amazon is divided into two branches at its mouth by the island of Marajo, the larger branch being ninety-six miles in width. About two thousand miles from its mouth it is upwards of a mile wide. So great is the force of this flood of water that it flows into the sea unmixed for nearly two hundred miles. The tide affects the river to a distance of about four hundred miles inland, and it is navigable from the sea for a distance of three thousand miles inland.

On the north bank of the Amazon there are ranges of low hills, partly bare and partly covered with thickets. These hills vary from three hundred to a thousand feet high, and extend about two hundred miles inland. Beyond them the shores of the river are low and flat for more than two thousand miles, till the spurs of the Andes are reached.

During the rainy season the Amazon overflows all its banks, like the Nile, for many hundreds of miles; during which season, as Martin Rattler truly remarked, the natives may be appropriately called aquatic animals. Towns and villages, and plantations belonging to Brazilians, foreign settlers, and half-civilized Indians, occur at intervals throughout the whole course of the river; and a little trade in dye-woods, india-rubber, medicinal drugs, Brazil nuts, coffee, etc., is done, but nothing to what might and ought to be, and perhaps would be, were this splendid country in the hands of an enterprising people. But the Amazonians are lazy, and the greater part of the resources of one of the richest countries in the world is totally neglected.

"Arrah!" said Barney, scratching his head and wrinkling his forehead intensely, as all that we have just written, and a great deal more, was told to him by a Scotch settler whom he found superintending a cattle estate and a saw-mill on the banks of the Amazon—"faix, then, I'm jist as wise now as before ye begun to spake. I've no head for fagures whatsumdiver; an' to tell me that the strame is ninety-six miles long and three thousand miles broad at the mouth, and sich like calcerlations, is o' no manner o' use, and jist goes in at wan ear an' out at the tother."

Whereupon the Scotch settler smiled and said, "Well, then, if ye can remember that the Amazon is longer than all Europe is broad; that it opens up to the ocean not less than ten thousand miles of the interior of Brazil; and that, *comparatively* speaking, no use is made of it whatever, ye'll remember enough to think about with profit for some time to come."

And Barney did think about it, and ponder it, and revolve it in his mind, for many days after, while he worked with Martin and the old trader at the paddles of their montaria. They found the work of canoeing easier than had been anticipated; for during the summer months the wind blows steadily up the river, and they were enabled to hoist their mat-sail and bowl along before it against the stream.

Hotels and inns there were none—for Brazil does not boast of many such conveniences, except in the chief towns—so they were obliged, in travelling, to make use of an empty hut or shed, when they chanced to stop at a village, and to cook their own victuals. More frequently, however, they preferred to encamp in the woods, slinging their hammocks between the stems of the trees, and making a fire sometimes, to frighten away the jaguars, which, although seldom seen, were often heard at night. They met large canoes and montarias occasionally coming down the stream, and saw them hauled up on shore, while their owners were cooking their breakfast in the woods; and once they came upon a solitary old Indian in a very curious position. They had entered a small stream in order to procure a few turtles' eggs, of which there were many in that place buried in the sand-banks. On turning a point where the stream was narrow and overhung with bushes and trees they beheld a canoe tied to the stem of a tree, and a hammock slung between two branches overhanging the water. In this an old Indian lay extended, quite naked and fast asleep! The old fellow had grown weary with paddling his little canoe, and finding the thicket along the river's banks so impenetrable that he could not land, he slung his hammock over the water, and thus quietly took his siesta. A flock of paroquets were screaming like little green demons just above him, and several alligators gave him a passing glance as they floundered heavily in the water below; but the red man cared not for such trifles. Almost involuntarily Martin began to hum the popular nursery rhyme,—

> "Hushy ba, baby, on the tree top;
> When the wind blows the cradle will rock."

"Arrah, if he was only two foot lower, its thirty pair o' long teeth would be stuck into his flank in wan minute, or I'm no prophet," said Barney, with a broad grin.

"Suppose we give him a touch with the paddle in passing," suggested Martin.

At this moment Barney started up, shaded his eyes with his hand, and after gazing for a few seconds at some object ahead of the canoe, he gave utterance to an exclamation of mingled surprise and consternation.

CHAPTER XV.

The great anaconda's dinner—Barney gets a fright—Turtles' eggs—A satisfactory "blow out"—Senhor Antonio's plantation—Preparations for a great hunt.

THE object which called forth the cry from our Irish friend, as related in the last chapter, was neither more nor less than a serpent of dimensions more enormous than Barney had ever before conceived of. It was upwards of sixteen feet long, and nearly as thick as a man's body; but about the neck it was three times that size. This serpent was not, indeed, of the largest size. In South America they grow to nearly forty feet in length. But it was fabulously gigantic in the eyes of our adventurers, who had never seen a serpent of any kind before.

"Oh!" cried Martin eagerly, "that must be an anaconda. Is it not?" he inquired, turning to the old trader.

"Yees; it dead," was the short reply.

"So it is!" cried Martin, who, on a nearer

approach, observed that the brute's body was cut in two just below the swelling at the neck.

"Now, did ye iver," cried Barney with increased surprise, "see a sarpint with a cow's horns growin' out at its mouth? Put ashore, old boy; we must have a 'vestigation o' this re-markable cratur."

The canoe was soon aground, and in another minute the three travellers were busily engaged in turning over the carcass of the huge reptile, which they found, to the amazement of Martin and Barney, had actually swallowed an ox whole, with the exception of the horns, which protruded from its mouth!

After much questioning, in bad Portuguese, broken English, and remarkable signs, Martin succeeded in drawing from the old trader the information that anacondas of a large size are often in the habit of thus bolting horses and oxen at a mouthful.

There is not the slightest exaggeration in this fact. Readers who are inclined to disbelieve it may refer to the works of Wallace and Gardner on Brazil —authorities which cannot be doubted.

The reptile commences by patiently watching until an unfortunate animal strays near to where it is lying, when it darts upon it, encircles it in its massive coils, and crushes it to death in an instant. Then it squeezes the body and broken bones into a shapeless mass; after which it licks the carcass all over, and covers it with a thick coating of saliva. Having thus prepared its mouthful, the anaconda begins at the tail and gradually engulfs its victim, while its elastic jaws, and throat, and stomach are distended sufficiently to let it in; after which it lies in a torpid state for many weeks, till the morsel is digested, when it is ready for another meal. A horse goes down entire, but a cow sticks at the horns, which the anaconda cannot swallow. They are allowed to protrude from its mouth until they decay and drop off.

They were at a loss at first to account for the creature being killed, but the old trader suggested that it had been found in a torpid state and slain by the Indian whom they had seen a short time ago enjoying his siesta among the trees.

Having cut it open, in order to convince themselves beyond a doubt that it had swallowed an entire ox, Martin and the old trader re-embarked in the canoe, and Barney was on the point of joining them when the bushes close beside him were slightly stirred. Looking quickly round, he beheld the head and the glittering eyes of another anaconda, apparently as large as the dead one, ready to dart upon him—at least so he fancied; but he did not wait to give it a chance. He fled instantly, and sprang towards the boat, which he nearly upset as he leaped into it, and pushed out into the stream. On reaching the middle of the river they looked back, but the anaconda was gone.

Soon after this they came to a long sand-bank, where the old trader said they should find as many turtles' eggs as they wished for, although to Barney and Martin there seemed to be nothing on the bank at all. The fresh-water turtle of the Amazon, of which there are various species, is one of the most useful of reptiles. Its flesh supplies abundance of good food; and the eggs, besides being eaten, afford an excellent oil. The largest species grow to the length of three feet, and have a flattish oval shell of a dark colour, and quite smooth. Turtles lay their eggs about the beginning of September, when the sand-banks begin to be uncovered. They scrape deep holes for them, and cover them carefully over, beating down the sand quite flat, and walking across the place several times, for the purpose of concealment. The eggs are then left to be hatched by the heat of the sun. But, alas for the poor turtles! men are too clever for them. The eggs are collected by the natives in thousands, and, when oil is to be made of them, they are thrown into a canoe, smashed and mixed up together, and left to stand, when the oil rises to the top, and is skimmed off and boiled. It keeps well, and is used both for lamps and cooking. Very few of the millions of eggs that are annually laid arrive at maturity.

When the young turtles issue forth and run to the water, there are many enemies watching for them. Great alligators open their jaws and swallow them by hundreds; jaguars come out of the forests and feed upon them; eagles and buzzards and wood ibises are there, too, to claim their share of the feast; and, if they are fortunate enough to escape all these, there are many large and ravenous fishes ready to seize them in the stream. It seems a marvel that any escape at all.

In a few minutes the old trader scraped up about a hundred eggs, to the immense satisfaction of Martin and Barney. Then he took a bow and arrow from the bottom of the montaria and shot a large turtle in the water, while his companions kindled a fire, intending to dine. Only the nose of the turtle was visible above water, but the old man was so expert in the use of the bow that he succeeded in transfixing the soft part of the animal's neck with an arrow, although that part was under water. It was a large turtle, and very fat and heavy, so that it was with difficulty the trader lifted it upon his old shoulders and bore it in triumph to the spot where his companions were busily engaged with their cooking operations. Turtles are frequently shot with the arrow by the natives; they are also taken in great numbers with the hook and the net.

Dinner was soon ready. Barney concocted an immense and savoury omelet, and the old trader cooked an excellent turtle-steak, while Martin prepared a junk of jaguar meat, which he roasted, being curious to taste it, as he had been told that the Indians like it very much. It was pretty good, but not equal to the turtles' eggs. The shell of the egg is leathery, and the yolk only is eaten. The Indians sometimes eat them raw, mixed with farina. Cakes of farina, and excellent coffee, concluded their repast; and Barney declared he had never had such a satisfactory "blow out" in his life; a sentiment with which Martin entirely agreed, and the old trader—if one might judge from the expression of his black countenance—sympathized.

For many weeks our adventurers continued to ascend the Amazon, sometimes sailing before the wind; at other times, when it fell calm, pushing the montaria up the current by means of long poles, or advancing more easily with the paddles. Occasionally they halted for a day at the residence of a wealthy cacao planter, in order to sell him some merchandise;

for which purpose the canoe was unloaded, and the bales were opened out for his inspection. Most of these planters were Brazilians, a few were Yankee adventurers, and one or two were Scotch and English; but nearly all had married Brazilian ladies, who, with their daughters, proved good customers to the old trader. Some of these ladies were extremely " purty craturs," as Barney expressed it; but most of them were totally uneducated and very ignorant—not knowing half so much as a child of seven or eight years old in more favoured lands. They were very fond of fine dresses and ornaments, of which considerable supplies were sent to them from Europe and the United States, in exchange for the valuable produce of their country. But, although their dresses were fine and themselves elegant, their houses were generally very poor affairs—made of wood and thatched with broad leaves; and it was no uncommon thing to see a lady, who seemed from her gay dress to be fitted for a drawing-room, seated on an earthen floor. But there were all sorts of extremes in this strange land; for at the next place they came to, perhaps, they found a population of Negroes and Indians, and most of the grown-up people were half naked, while all the children were entirely so.

At one plantation, where they resolved to spend a

few days, the owner had a pond which was much frequented by alligators. These he was in the habit of hunting periodically, for the sake of their fat, which he converted into oil. At the time of their arrival he was on the eve of starting on a hunting expedition to the lake, which was about eight miles distant; so Barney and Martin determined to go and " see the fun," as the latter said.

" Martin, lad," remarked Barney, as they followed the Negro slave who had been sent by Senhor Antonio, the planter, to conduct them to the lake, while he remained behind for an hour or two to examine the bales of the old trader, " this is the quarest country, I believe, that iver was made. What with bastes, and varmints, and riptiles, and traes, and bushes, and rivers, it bates all creation."

" Certainly it does, Barney; and it is a pity there are so few people in it who know how to make use of the things that are scattered all around them. I'm inclined to think the hermit was right when he said that they wanted the Bible. They are too far sunk in laziness and idleness to be raised up by anything else. Just look," continued Martin, glancing round, " what a wonderful place this is! It seems as if all the birds and curious trees in Brazil had congregated here to meet us."

"So't does," said Barney, stopping to gaze on the scene through which they were passing, with an expression of perplexity on his face, as if he found the sight rather too much even for *his* comprehension. Besides the parrots and scarlet and yellow macaws, and other strange-looking birds which we have elsewhere mentioned, there were long-tailed light-coloured cuckoos flying about from tree to tree, not calling like the cuckoo of Europe at all, but giving forth a sound like the creaking of a rusty hinge; there were hawks and buzzards of many different kinds, and red-breasted orioles in the bushes, and black vultures flying overhead, and Muscovy ducks sweeping past with whizzing wings, and flocks of the great wood-ibis sailing in the air on noiseless pinions, and hundreds of other birds that it would require an ornithologist to name; and myriads of insects—especially ants and spiders, great and small—that no entomologist could chronicle in a life-time,—all these were heard and seen at once; while of the animals that were heard, but not so often seen, there were black and spotted jaguars, and pacas, and cotias, and armadillos, and deer, and many others that would take *pages* to enumerate and whole books to describe.

But the noise was the great point. That was the thing that took Martin and Barney quite aback, although it was by no means new to them; but they could not get used to it. And no wonder! Ten thousand paroquets shrieking passionately, like a hundred knife-grinders at work, is no joke; especially when their melodies are mingled with the discordant cries of herons, and bitterns, and cranes, and the ceaseless buzz and hum of insects, like the bagpipe's drone, and the dismal croaking of boat-bills and frogs—one kind of which latter, by the way, doesn't croak at all, but *whistles*, ay, better than many a bird! The universal hubbub is tremendous. I tell you, reader, that you *don't* understand it, and you *can't* understand it; and if, after I had used the utmost excess of exaggerated language to convey a correct impression of the reality, you were to imagine that you really *did* understand it, you would be very lamentably mistaken—that's all!

Nevertheless, you must not run away with the idea that the whole empire of Brazil is like this. There are dark thick solitudes in these vast forests which are solemn and silent enough at times, and there are wide grassy campos and great sandy plains where such sounds are absent. Yet there are also thousands of such spots as I have just described, where all nature, in earth, air, and water, is instinct with noisy animal life.

After two hours' walk, Martin and his companion reached the lake, and here active preparations were making for the alligator hunt.

"Is that the only place ye have to spind the night in, Sambo?" said Barney to their conductor, as he pointed to a wooden shed near which some fifteen or twenty Negro slaves were overhauling the fishing tackle.

"Yis, massa," answered the black, showing his white teeth; "dat is de hottle of dis great city." Sambo could speak a little English, having wrought for several years on the coffee plantation of a Yankee settler. He was a bit of a wag, too, much to the indignation of his grave master, the Senhor Antonio, who abhorred jesting.

"Ye're too cliver, avic," said Barney, with a patronizing smile; "take care ye don't use up yer intellect too fast. It hurts the constitution in the long-run."

"I say, Barney," cried Martin, who had gone ahead of his companions, "come here, man, and just look at this pond. It's literally crammed full of alligators."

"Musha, but there's more alligators than wather, I belave!" exclaimed Barney.

The pond was indeed swarming with these ferocious reptiles, which were constantly thrusting their ugly snouts above the surface, and then disappearing with a flourish of their powerful tails. During the rainy season this lake was much larger, and afforded ample room for its inhabitants; but at the height of the dry season, which it was at this time, there was little water, and it was much overstocked. When alligators are thus put upon short allowance of water they frequently bury themselves in the wet mud, and lie dormant for a long time, while the water continues to retire and leaves them buried. But when the first shower of the rainy season falls, they burst open their tomb and drag their dry bodies to the lake or river on whose margin they went to sleep.

An hour or two later the Senhor Antonio arrived, but as it was getting dark nothing could be done until the following morning; so they slung their hammocks under the wooden shed on the margin of the lake, and, in order to save themselves as much as possible from the bites of the tormenting mosquitoes, went to sleep with their heads tied up in their handkerchiefs and their hands thrust into their breeches pockets! The occasional splash and snort of contending alligators, about twenty yards off, varied the monotony of the hours of darkness, while the frogs and cranes and jaguars sang their lullaby.

CHAPTER XVI.

An alligator hunt—Remarkable explosions—The rainy season ushered in by an awful resurrection.

AT sunrise an expressive shout in Portuguese set the black slaves on their feet, and after a hasty breakfast of alligator-tail and farina they commenced operations. Alligator-tail is by no means bad food, and after the first mouthful—taken with hesitation and swallowed with difficulty—Martin and Barney both pronounced it "capital." Sambo, who had cooked the delicate morsel, and stood watching them, smacked his lips and added, "Fuss-rate."

All being now ready for the hunt, a number of Negroes entered the water, which was nowhere very deep, with long poles in their hands. This appeared to Martin and Barney a very reckless and dangerous thing to do, as no doubt it was. Nevertheless, accidents, they were told, very rarely happened.

Sambo, who was the overseer of the party, was the first to dash up to the middle in the water. "Hi," exclaimed that dingy individual, making a torrent of remarks in Portuguese, while he darted his long pole hither and thither; then, observing that Martin and Barney were gazing at him open-mouthed, he shouted, "Look out, boys! here 'im comes! Take care, ole feller, or he jump right down you' throat! hi-i-i!"

As he spoke, a large alligator, having been rudely stirred up from his muddy bed, floundered on the surface of the lake, and Sambo instantly gave it a thump over the back and a blow under the ribs, which had the effect of driving it in the direction of the shore. Here a number of Negroes were ready for him, and the moment he came within reach a coil of rope with a noose on the end of it, called a lasso, was adroitly thrown over the reptile's head; ten or twelve men then hauled the lasso and dragged it ashore amid shouts of triumph. This alligator was twenty feet long, with an enormous misshapen head and fearful rows of teeth that were terrible to behold. The monster did not submit to be captured, however, without a struggle; and the Negroes grew wild with excitement as they yelled and leaped madly about, seeking to avoid its dangerous jaws and the blows of its powerful tail. After some trouble, a second lasso was thrown over the tail, which was thus somewhat restrained in its 'movements; and Sambo, approaching cautiously with an axe, cut a deep gash just at the root of that formidable appendage, which rendered it harmless. "Hi-i," shouted Sambo in triumph, as he sprang towards the animal's head and inflicted a similar gash in the neck; "dare, you quite finish, ole feller."

"Musha, but that's thrue!" ejaculated Barney, who stood staring at the whole proceeding like one in a trance. "Did ye iver git a bite, Sambo?"

Barney received no answer, for his sable friend was already up to his waist in the water with five or six of his brethren, who were flourishing their long poles and driving the snorting alligators towards the shore, where their comrades, with lassos and harpoons, awaited them. Sometimes they harpooned the alligators, and then fastening lassos to their heads and tails, or to a hind leg, dragged them ashore; at other times they threw the lasso over their heads at once, without taking the trouble to harpoon them. It was a terrible and a wonderful sight to witness the Negroes in the very midst of a shoal of these creatures, any one of which could have taken a man into his jaws quite easily, whence, once between these long saw-like rows of teeth, no man could have escaped to tell how sharp they were. The creatures were so numerous that it was impossible to thrust a pole into the mud without stirring up one of them; but they were so terrified at the sudden attack and the shouts of the Negroes, that they thought only of escape.

Suddenly there arose a great cry. One of the lassos had snapped, and the alligator was floundering back into the water, when Sambo rushed in up to the armpits and caught the end of the rope. At the same moment two alligators made at the Negro with open jaws. It is probable that the animals went in his direction by mere accident, and would have brushed past him in blind haste; but to Martin and Barney it seemed as if the poor man's fate were sealed, and they uttered a loud shout of horror as they bounded simultaneously into the water, not knowing what to do, but being unable to restrain the impulse to spring to Sambo's aid. Fortunately, however, one of the other Negroes was near Sambo. He sprang forward and dealt the alligators two tremendous blows with his pole on their snouts, right and left, which turned them off. Then other Negroes came up, laid hold of Sambo, who would not let go his hold and was being dragged into deep water, caught the end of the rope, and in ten minutes hauled their victim to the shore, where it was quickly despatched in the usual manner.

By this time about a dozen alligators, varying from ten to twenty feet in length, had been captured; and

Barney at length became so bold that he requested to be allowed to try his hand at throwing the lasso, the dexterous use of which by the Negroes had filled him with admiration. A loud burst of laughter greeted this proposal, and Sambo showed a set of teeth that might have made even the alligators envious, as he handed the Irishman a coil of line.

"Now don't miss, Barney," cried Martin, laughing heartily, as his comrade advanced to the edge of the lake and watched his opportunity. "Mind, your credit as an expert hunter is at stake."

The Senhor Antonio stood close behind the Irishman, with his arms folded, and a sarcastic smile on his countenance.

"Don't send it down him's throat," yelled Sambo. "Hi-i; dat's de vay to swing um round. Stir um up, boys!—poke um up, villains, hi!"

The Negroes in the water obeyed with frantic glee, and the terrified monsters surged about in all directions, so that Barney found it almost impossible to fix his attention on any particular individual. At length he made up his mind, whirled the coil round his head, discharged the noose, caught the Senhor Antonio round the neck, and jerked him violently to the ground!

There was a simultaneous pause of horror among

the slaves; but it was too much for their risible faculties to withstand. With one accord they rushed howling into the water to conceal their laughter, and began to stir up and belabour the alligators with their poles, until the surface of the lake was a sheet of foam.

Meanwhile the Senhor Antonio sprang to his feet and began to bluster considerably in Portuguese; but poor Barney seemed awfully crestfallen, and the deep concern which wrinkled his face, and the genuine regret that sounded in the tones of his voice, at length soothed the indignant Brazilian, who frowned gravely, and waving his hand, as if to signify that Barney had his forgiveness, he stalked up to the shed, lighted a cigarito, and lay down in his hammock.

"Well!" said Martin in an under-tone, "you did it that time, Barney. I verily thought the old fellow was hanged. He became quite livid in the face."

"Och! bad luck to the lasso, say I. May I niver more see the swate groves o' Killarney if iver I meddle with wan again."

"Hi-i; you is fuss-rate," said Sambo, as he and his comrades returned and busied themselves in cutting up the dead alligators. "You beat de Niggers all to not'ing. Not any of dis yere chiles eber lasso Sen'or Antonio yet; no, neber!"

It was some time before the Negroes could effectually subdue their merriment, but at length they succeeded, and applied themselves vigorously to the work of cutting out the fat. The alligators were all cut open, a work of no small difficulty owing to the hard scales which covered them as with coats of mail; then the fat, which accumulates in large quantities about the intestines, was cut out and made up into packets in the skins of the smaller ones, which were taken off for this purpose.

These packets were afterwards carried to the senhor's dwelling, and the fat melted down into oil, which served for burning in lamps quite as well as train oil. The flesh of a smaller species of alligator, some of which were also taken, is considered excellent food; and while the Negroes were engaged in their work, Barney made himself useful by kindling a large fire and preparing a savoury dish for "all hands," plentifully seasoned with salt and pepper, with which condiments the country is well supplied, and of which the people are exceedingly fond.

There was also caught in this lake a large species of fish called pirarucu, which, strangely enough, found it possible to exist in spite of alligators. They were splendid creatures, from five to six feet long, and covered with large scales more than an inch in diameter, which were beautifully marked and spotted with red. These fish were most delicately flavoured, and Barney exerted his talents to the utmost in order to do them justice. Martin also did his best to prove himself a willing and efficient assistant, and cleaned and washed the pirarucu steaks and the junks of alligator-tail to admiration. In short, the exertions of the two strangers in this way quite won the hearts of the Negroes, and after dinner the Senhor Antonio had quite recovered his good-humour.

While staying at this place Martin had an opportunity of seeing a great variety of the curious fish with which the Amazon is stocked. These are so numerous that sometimes, when sailing up stream with a fair wind, they were seen leaping all round the canoe in shoals, so that it was only necessary to strike the water with the paddles in order to kill a few.

The peixe boi, or cow-fish, is one of the most curious of the inhabitants of the Amazon. It is about six feet long, and no less than five feet in circumference at its thickest part. It is a perfectly smooth and what we may call *dumpy* fish, of a leaden colour, with a semicircular flat tail, and a large mouth with thick fleshy lips, resembling those of a cow. There are stiff bristles on the lips, and a few scattered hairs over the body. It has two fins just behind the head, and below these, in the females, there are two breasts, from which good white milk flows when pressure is applied. The cow-fish feeds on grass at the borders of rivers and lakes; and when suckling its young, it carries it in its fins or flippers, and clasps the little one to its breast, just as a mother clasps her baby! It is harpooned and taken for the sake of its fat, from which oil is made. The flesh is also very good, resembling beef in quality, and it was much relished by Martin and Barney, who frequently dined on beef-steaks cut from this remarkable cow-fish.

There was also another fish which surprised our adventurers not a little the first time they met with it. One evening Senhor Antonio had ordered a net to be thrown into the river, being desirous of procuring a few fresh fish for the use of his establishment. The Indians and Negroes soon after commenced dragging, and in a few minutes afterwards the sandy bank of the river was strown with an immense variety of small fish, among which were a few of a larger kind. Martin and Barney became excited as they saw them leaping and spluttering about, and ran in amongst them to assist in gathering them into baskets. But scarcely had the latter advanced a few steps when there was a loud report, as if a pistol had gone off under his feet.

"Hallo!" exclaimed the Irishman, leaping two feet into the air. On his reaching the ground again a similar explosion occurred, and Barney dashed aside, overturning Martin in his haste. Martin's heel caught on a stone, and he fell flat on the ground, when instantly there was a report as if he had fallen upon and burst an inflated paper bag. The natives laughed loud and long, while the unfortunate couple sprang up the bank, half inclined to think that an earthquake was about to take place. The cause of their fright was then pointed out. It was a species of small fish which has the power of inflating the fore part of its body into a complete ball, and which, when stamped upon, explodes with a loud noise. There were great numbers of these scattered among the other fish, and also large quantities of a little fish armed with long spines, which inflict a serious wound when trodden upon.

At this place adventures on a small scale crowded upon our travellers so thickly that Martin began to look upon sudden surprises as a necessary of life, and Barney said that "if it wint on any longer he feared his eyebrows would get fixed near the top of his head, and niver more come down."

One evening, soon after their departure from the residence of Senhor Antonio, the old trader was sitting steering in the stern of his canoe, which was running up before a pretty stiff breeze. Martin was lying on his back, as was his wont in such easy circumstances, amusing himself with Marmoset, and Barney was reclining in the bow talking solemnly to Grampus, when suddenly the wind ceased and it became a dead calm. The current was so strong that they could scarcely paddle against it, so they resolved to go no further that night, and ran the canoe ashore on a low point of mud, intending to encamp under the trees, no human habitation being near them. The mud-bank was hard and dry, and cracked with the heat, for it was now the end of the dry season, and the river had long since retired from it.

"Not a very comfortable place, Barney," said Martin, looking round, as he threw down one of the bales which he had just carried up from the canoe. "Hallo! there's a hut, I declare. Come, that's a comfort anyhow."

As he spoke Martin pointed to one of the solitary and rudely-constructed huts or sheds which the natives of the banks of the Amazon sometimes erect during the dry season and forsake when the river overflows its banks. The hut was a very old one, and had evidently been inundated, for the floor was a mass of dry, solid mud, and the palm-leaf roof was much damaged. However, it was better than nothing, so they slung their hammocks under it, kindled a fire, and prepared supper. While they were busy discussing this meal, a few dark and ominous clouds gathered in the sky, and the old trader, glancing uneasily about him, gave them to understand that he feared the rainy season was going to begin.

"Well, then," said Barney, lighting his pipe and stretching himself at full length in his hammock, with a leg swinging to and fro over one side and his head leaning over the other, as was his wont when he felt particularly comfortable in mind and body— "well then, avic, let it begin. If we're sure to have it anyhow, the sooner it begins the better, to my thinkin'."

"I don't know that," said Martin, who was seated on a large stone beside the fire sipping a can of coffee, which he shared equally with Marmoset. The monkey sat on his shoulder gazing anxiously into his face, with an expression that seemed as if the creature were mentally exclaiming, "Now me, now you; now me, now you," during the whole process. "It would be better, I think, if we were in a more sheltered position before it begins. Ha! there it comes though, in earnest."

A smart shower began to fall as he spoke, and

percolating through the old roof, descended rather copiously on the mud floor. In a few minutes there was a heaving of the ground under their feet!

"Ochone!" cried Barney, taking his pipe out of his mouth and looking down with a disturbed expression, "there's an arthquake, I do belave."

For a few seconds there was a dead silence.

"Nonsense," whispered Martin uneasily.

"It's dramin' I must have been," sighed Barney, resuming his pipe.

Again the ground heaved and cracked, and Martin and the old trader had just time to spring to their feet when the mud floor of the hut burst upwards and a huge, dried-up-looking alligator crawled forth, as if from the bowels of the earth! It glanced up at Barney, opened its tremendous jaws, and made as if it would run at the terrified old trader; then, observing the doorway, it waddled out and, trundling down the bank, plunged into the river and disappeared.

Barney could find no words to express his feelings, but continued to gaze with an unbelieving expression down into the hole out of which the monster had come, and in which it had buried itself many weeks before, when the whole country was covered with soft mud. At that time it had probably regarded the shelter of the inundated hut as of some advantage, and had lain down to repose. The water retiring had left it there buried, and—as we have already mentioned in reference to alligators—when the first shower of the rainy season fell it was led by instinct to burst its earthy prison and seek its native element.

Before Barney or his companions could recover from their surprise, they had other and more urgent matters to think about. The dark clouds burst overhead, and the rain descended like a continued waterspout—not in drops, but in heavy sheets and masses. The roof of the hut gave way in several places, driving them into a corner for shelter; the river began to rise rapidly, soon flooding the hut; and when darkness overspread the land, they found themselves drenched to the skin and suspended in their hammocks over a running stream of water!

This event brought about an entire change in the aspect of nature, and was the cause of a sad and momentous era in the adventures of Martin Rattler and his companion.

CHAPTER XVII.

The Gapo—Interruptions—Grampus and Marmoset—Canoeing in the woods—A night on a floating island.

THERE is a peculiar and very striking feature in the character of the great Amazon, which affects the distinctive appearance of that river and materially alters the manners and customs of those who dwell beside it. This peculiarity is the periodical overflow of its low banks; and the part thus overflowed is called the *Gapo*. It extends from a little above the town of Santarem up to the confines of Peru, a distance of about seventeen hundred miles, and varies in width from one to twenty miles; so that the country when inundated assumes in many places the appearance of an extensive lake with forest trees growing out of the water, and travellers may proceed many hundreds of miles in their canoes without once entering the main stream of the river. At this time the natives become almost aquatic animals. Several tribes of Indians inhabit the Gapo, such as the Purupurus, Muras, and others. They build small movable huts on the sandy shores during the dry season, and on rafts in the wet. They subsist on turtle, cow-fish, and the other fish with which the river abounds, and live almost entirely in their canoes; while at night they frequently sling their hammocks between the branches of trees and sleep suspended over the deep water.

Some of the animals found in the Gapo are peculiar to it, being attracted by the fruit-trees which are found growing only there. The Indians assert that every tree that grows in the Gapo is distinct from all those that grow in other districts; and when we consider that these trees are submerged for six months every year, till they are tall enough to rise above the highest water-level, we may well believe their constitution is somewhat different from those that are reared on ordinary ground. The Indians are wonderfully expert in finding their way among the trackless mazes of the Gapo, being guided by the broken twigs and scraped bark that indicate the route followed by previous travellers.

Owing to this sudden commencement of the rainy season, the old trader resolved to return to a small village and there spend several months. Martin and Barney were much annoyed at this; for the former was impatient to penetrate farther into the interior; and the latter had firmly made up his mind to visit the diamond mines, about which he entertained the most extravagant notions. He did not, indeed, know in the least how to get to these mines, nor even in which direction they lay; but he had a strong impression that as long as he continued travelling he was approaching gradually nearer to them, and he had no doubt whatever that he would get to them at last. It was therefore with no small degree of impatience that they awaited the pleasure of their sable master, who explained to them that when the waters reached their height he would proceed.

Everything comes to an end, even a long story. After many weeks had passed slowly by, their sojourn in this village came to an end too. It was a dull place, very dull, and they had nothing to do; and the few poor people who lived there seemed to have very little or nothing to do. We will therefore pass it over, and resume our narrative at the point when the old trader announced to Barney that the flood was at its height and they would now continue their journey. They embarked once more in their old canoe with their goods and chattels, not forgetting Marmoset and Grampus, whose friendship during their inactive life had become more close than ever. This friendship was evidenced chiefly by the matter-of-course way in which Grampus permitted the monkey to mount his back and ride about the village and through the woods, where dry places could be found, as long as she pleased. Marmoset was fonder of riding than walking, so that Grampus had enough to do; but he did not put himself much about. He trotted, walked, galloped, and lay down when and where and as often as he chose, without any reference to the small monkey; and Marmoset held on through thick and thin, and nibbled nuts or whatever else it picked up, utterly regardless of where it was going to or the pace at which it went. It was sharp, though, that small monkey, sharp as a needle, and had its little black eyes glancing on all sides; so that when Grampus dashed through underwood, and the branches threatened to sweep it off, it ducked its head, or, lying flat down, shut its eyes and held on with all its teeth and four hands like a limpet to a rock. Marmoset was not careful as to her attitude on dog-back. She sat with her face to the front or the rear, just as her fancy or convenience dictated.

After leaving the village they travelled for many days and nights through the Gapo. Although afloat on the waters of the Amazon, they never entered the main river after the first few days, but wound their way, in a creeping, serpentine sort of fashion, through small streams and lakes and swamps, from which the light was partially excluded by the thick foliage of the forest. It was a strange scene that illimitable watery waste, and aroused new sensations in the breasts of our travellers. As Barney said, it made him "feel quite solemn-like and eerie to travel through the woods by wather."

The canoe was forced under branches and among dense bushes till they got into a part where the trees were loftier and a deep gloom prevailed. Here the lowest branches were on a level with the surface of the water, and many of them were putting forth beautiful flowers. On one occasion they came to a grove of small palms, which were so deep in the water that the leaves were only a few feet above the surface. Indeed, they were so low that one of them caught Martin's straw-hat and swept it overboard.

"Hallo! stop!" cried Martin, interrupting the silence so suddenly that Grampus sprang up with a growl, under the impression that game was in view, and Marmoset scampered off behind a packing-box with an angry shriek.

"What's wrong, lad?" inquired Barney.

"Back water, quick! my hat's overboard, and

there's an alligator going to snap it up. Look alive, man!"

In a few seconds the canoe was backed and the straw-hat rescued from its perilous position.

"It's an ill wind that blows nae guid, as the Scotch say," remarked Barney, rising in the canoe and reaching towards something among the overhanging branches. "Here's wan o' them trees that old black-face calls a maraja, with some splendid bunches o' fruit on it. Hould yer hat, Martin; there's more nor enough for supper anyhow."

As he spoke, a rustling in the leaves told that monkeys were watching them, and Marmoset kept peeping up as if she half expected they might be relations. But the moment the travellers caught sight of them they bounded away screaming.

Having gathered as much fruit as they required, they continued their voyage, and presently emerged into the pleasant sunshine in a large grassy lake, which was filled with lilies and beautiful water-plants, little yellow bladder-worts, with several other plants of which they knew not the names, especially one with a thick swollen stalk, curious leaves, and bright-blue flowers. This lake was soon passed, and they again entered into the gloomy forest, and paddled among the lofty trunks of the trees, which rose like massive columns out of the deep water. There was enough of animal life there, however, to amuse and interest them. The constant plash of falling fruit showed that birds were feeding overhead. Sometimes a flock of parrots or bright-blue chatterers swept from tree to tree, or a trogon swooped at a falling bunch of fruit and caught it ere it reached the water; while ungainly toucans plumped clumsily down upon the branches, and sat, in striking contrast, beside the lovely pompadours, with their claret-coloured plumage and delicate white wings.

Vieing with these birds in splendour were several large bright-yellow flowers of the creeping-plants which twined round the trees. Some of these plants had white, spotted, and purple blossoms; and there was one splendid species, called by the natives the *flor de Santa Anna*—the flower of St. Ann—which emitted a delightful odour, and was four inches in diameter.

Having traversed this part of the wood, they once more emerged upon the main stream of the Amazon. It was covered with water-fowl. Large logs of trees and numerous floating islands of grass were sailing down; and on these sat hundreds of white gulls, demurely and comfortably voyaging to the ocean, for the sea would be their final resting-place if they sat on these logs and islands until they descended several hundreds of miles of the great river.

"I wish," said Martin, after a long silence, during which the travellers had been gazing on the watery waste as they paddled up stream—"I wish that we could fall in with solid land, where we might have something cooked. I'm desperately hungry now; but I don't see a spot of earth large enough for a mosquito to rest his foot on."

"We'll jist have to take to farhina and wather," remarked Barney, laying down his paddle and proceeding leisurely to light his pipe. "It's a blissin' we've got baccy, anyhow. 'Tis mesilf that could niver git on without it."

"I wish you joy of it, Barney. It may fill your mouth, but it can't stop your hunger."

"Och, boy, it's little ye know. Sure it stops the cravin's o' hunger, and kapes yer stumick from callin' out for iver, till ye fall in with somethin' to ate."

"It does not seem to stop the mouth, then, Barney, for you call out for grub oftener than I do. And then you say that you couldn't get on without it, so you're a slave to it, old boy. I wouldn't be a slave to anything if I could help it."

"Martin, lad, ye're gittin' deep. Take care now, or ye'll be in mettlefeesics soon.—I say, ould black-face,"—Barney was not on ceremony with the old trader,—" is there no land in thim parts at all?"

" No, not dis night."

" Och, then, we'll have to git up a tree and try to cook somethin' there, for I'm not goin' to work on flour and wather. Hallo! hould on! There's an island, or the portrait o' wan. Port your helm, Naygur! hard aport! D'ye hear?"

The old man heard, but, as usual, paid no attention to the Irishman's remarks, and the canoe would have passed straight on, had not Barney used his bow-paddle so energetically that he managed to steer her, as he expressed it, by the nose, and ran her against a mass of floating logs which had caught firmly in a thicket, and were so covered with grass and broken twigs as to have very much the appearance of a real island. Here they landed, so to speak, kindled a small fire, made some coffee, roasted a few fish, baked several cakes, and were soon as happy and comfortable as hungry and wearied men usually are when they obtain rest and food.

" This is what I call jolly," remarked Barney.

" What's jolly?" inquired Martin.

" Why, *this*, to be sure—grub to begin with, and a smoke and a convenient snooze in prospect."

The hopes which Barney cherished, however, were

destined to be blighted, at least in part. To the victuals he did ample justice ; the pipe was delightful and in good working order; but when they lay down to repose, they were attacked by swarms of stinging ants, which the heat of the fire had driven out of the old logs. These and mosquitoes effectually banished sleep from their eyelids, and caused them to reflect very seriously, and to state to each other more than once very impressively, that, with all their beauties and wonders, tropical lands had their disadvantages, and there was no place like the "ould country" after all.

CHAPTER XVIII.

The sad and momentous era referred to at the close of the chapter preceding the last.

ONE sultry evening, many weeks after our travellers had passed the uncomfortable night on the floating island in the Gapo, they came to a place where the banks of the river rose boldly up in rugged rocks and hemmed in the waters of the Amazon, which were by this time somewhat abated. Here they put ashore, intending to kindle their fire and encamp for the night, having been up and hard at work since daybreak.

The evening was calm and beautiful, and the troublesome insects not so numerous as usual—probably owing to the nature of the ground. One or two monkeys showed themselves for a moment, as if to inquire who was there, and then ran away screaming; a porcupine also crossed their path, and several small bright snakes, of a harmless species, glided over the rocks, and sought refuge among the small bushes;

but beyond these there were few of the sights and sounds that were wont to greet them in the forest.

"I think things look well to-night," remarked Martin, as he threw down a bundle of sticks which he had gathered for the fire; "we shall have a comfortable snooze for certain, if the mosquitoes don't wake up."

"I'm not so sure of that," remarked Barney, striking a light with flint and steel, and stooping to puff the smouldering spark into a flame. "I've larned by exparience that ye niver can be "—puff—" sure o' nothin' in this "—puff—" remarkable country. Jist look at Darkey now," continued the Irishman, sitting down on a stone before the fire, which now began to kindle up, and stuffing the tobacco into his pipe with his little finger. "There he is, a livin' Naygur, aliftin' of the provision-bag out o' the canoe. Well, if he was all of a suddent to turn into Marmoset an' swaller himself, an' then jump down the throat of Grampus, and the whole consarn, canoe and all, to disappear, I don't think that I would be much surprised."

"Would you not, Barney? I suspect that I should be a little, under the circumstances; perhaps the old Nigger would be more so."

"Niver a taste," continued Barney. "Ye see, if

that was to happen, I would then know that it was all a drame. I've more than wance expected to wake up since I comed into furrin parts; the only thing that kapes me in doubt about it is the baccy."

"How so, Barney?"

"Why, bekase it tastes so rael, good luck to it! that I can't git myself to think it's only a drame. Jist look, now," he continued, in the same tone of voice; "if it wasn't a drame, how could I see sich a thing as that standin' on the rock over there?"

Martin glanced towards the spot pointed out by his friend, and immediately started up with surprise.

"Hallo, Barney! that's no dream, I'll vouch for it. He's an Indian, and a very ugly one, too, I declare.— I say, old fellow, do you know what sort of savage that is?"

"Not know," answered the trader, glancing uneasily at the stranger.

"He might have the dacency to put on more cloes, anyhow," muttered Barney, as he gazed inquiringly at the savage.

The being who had thus appeared so suddenly before the travellers belonged to one of the numerous tribes of Indians inhabiting the country near the head-waters of some of the chief tributaries of the Amazon. He was almost entirely naked, having merely a scanty covering on his loins, and carried a small quiver full of arrows at his back, and what appeared to be a long spear in his hand. His figure was strongly but not well formed, and his face, which was of a dark copper hue, was disfigured in a most remarkable manner. A mass of coarse black hair formed the only covering to his head. His cheeks were painted with curious marks of jet black. But the most remarkable points about him were the huge pieces of wood which formed ornaments in his ears and under lip. They were round and flat, like the wooden wheel of a toy-cart, about half an inch thick, and larger than an old-fashioned watch. These were fitted into enormous slits made in the ears and under lip, and the latter projected more than two inches from his mouth! Indeed, the cut that had been made to receive this ornament was so large that the lip had been almost cut off altogether, and merely hung by each corner of his mouth! The aspect of the man was very hideous, and it was by no means improved when, having recovered from his surprise at unexpectedly encountering strangers, he opened his mouth to the full extent and uttered a savage yell.

The cry was answered immediately. In a few minutes a troop of upwards of thirty savages sprang from the woods, and ascending the rock on which their comrade stood, gazed down on the travellers in surprise, and, by their movements, seemed to be making hasty preparations for an attack.

By this time Barney had recovered his self-possession, and became thoroughly convinced of the reality of the apparition before him. Drawing his pistol hastily from his belt, he caught up a handful of gravel, wherewith he loaded it to the muzzle, ramming down the charge with a bit of mandioca cake in lieu of a wad; then drawing his cutlass he handed it to Martin, exclaiming, "Come, lad; we're in for it now. Take you the cutlass, and I'll try their skulls with the butt o' my pistol; it has done good work before now in that way. If there's no more o' the blackguards in the background, we'll bate them aisy."

Martin instinctively grasped the cutlass, and there is no doubt that, under the impulse of that remarkable quality, British valour, which utterly despises odds, they would have hurled themselves recklessly upon the savages, when the horrified old trader threw himself on Barney's neck and implored him not to fight; for if he did they would all be killed, and if he only kept quiet the savages would perhaps do them no harm. At the same moment about fifty additional Indians arrived upon the scene of action. This, and the old man's earnest entreaties, induced them to hesitate for an instant, and before they could determine what to do, they were surprised by some of the savages, who rushed upon them from behind and took them prisoners. Barney struggled long and fiercely, but he was at length overpowered by numbers. The pistol, which missed fire, was wrenched from his grasp, and his hands were speedily bound behind his back. Martin was likewise disarmed and secured; not, however, before he made a desperate slash at one of the savages, which narrowly missed his skull, and cut away his lip ornament.

As for the old trader, he made no resistance at all, but submitted quietly to his fate. The savages did not seem to think it worth their while to bind him. Grampus bounced and barked round the party savagely, but did not attack; and Marmoset slept in the canoe in blissful ignorance of the whole transaction.

The hands of the two prisoners being firmly bound, they were allowed to do as they pleased; so they sat down on a rock in gloomy silence, and watched the naked savages as they rifled the canoe and danced joyfully round the treasures which their active knives and fingers soon exposed to view. The old trader took things philosophically. Knowing that it was absolutely impossible to escape, he sat quietly down on a stone, rested his chin on his hands, heaved one or two deep sighs, and thereafter seemed to be nothing more than an ebony statue.

The ransacking of the canoe and appropriating of its contents occupied the savages but a short time, after which they packed everything up in small bundles, which they strapped upon their backs. Then, making signs to their prisoners to rise, they all marched away into the forest. Just as they were departing, Marmoset, observing that she was about to be left behind, uttered a frantic cry, which brought Grampus gambolling to her side. With an active bound the monkey mounted its charger, and away they went into the forest in the track of the band of savages.

During the first part of their march Martin and Barney were permitted to walk beside each other, and they conversed in low, anxious tones.

"Surely," said Barney, as they marched along surrounded by Indians, "thim long poles the savages have got are not spears; I don't see no point to them."

"And what's more remarkable," added Martin, "is that they all carry quivers full of arrows, but none of them have bows."

"There's a raison for iverything," said Barney, pointing to one of the Indians in advance; "that fellow explains the mystery."

As he spoke, the savage referred to lowered the pole, which seemed to be about thirteen feet long, and pushing an arrow into a hole in the end of it, applied it to his mouth. In another moment the arrow flew through the air and grazed a bird that was sitting on a branch hard by.

"'Tis a blow-pipe, and no mistake!" cried Barney.

"And a poisoned arrow, I'm quite sure," added Martin; "for it only ruffled the bird's feathers, and see, it has fallen to the ground."

"Och, then, but we'd have stood a bad chance in a fight, if thim's the wipons they use. Och, the dirty spalpeens! Martin, dear, we're done for. There's no chance for us at all."

This impression seemed to take such deep hold of Barney's mind, that his usually reckless and half jesting disposition was completely subdued, and he walked along in gloomy silence, while a feeling of deep dejection filled the heart of his young companion.

The blow-pipe which these Indians use is an ingeniously contrived weapon. It is made from a species of palm-tree. When an Indian wants one, he goes into the woods and selects a tree with a long slender stem of less than an inch in diameter. He extracts the pith out of this; and then cuts another stem, so much larger than the first that he can push the small tube into the bore of the large one—thus the slight bend in one is counteracted by the other, and a perfectly straight pipe is formed. The mouthpiece is afterwards neatly finished off. The arrows used are very short, having a little ball of cotton at the end to fill the tube of the blow-pipe. The points are dipped in a peculiar poison, which has the effect of producing death when introduced into the blood by a mere scratch of the skin. The Indians can send these arrows an immense distance, and with unerring aim, as Martin and Barney had many an opportunity of witnessing during their long and weary journey on foot to the forest-home of the savages.

CHAPTER XIX.

Worse and worse—Everything seems to go wrong together.

ALTHOUGH the Indians did not maltreat the unfortunate strangers who had thus fallen into their hands, they made them proceed by forced marches through the wilderness; and as neither Barney nor Martin had been of late much used to long walks, they felt the journey very severely. The old trader had been accustomed to everything wretched and unfortunate and uncomfortable from his childhood, so he plodded onward in silent indifference.

The country through which they passed became every day more and more rugged, until at length it assumed the character of a wild mountainous district. Sometimes they wound their way in a zigzag manner up the mountain sides, by paths so narrow that they could scarcely find a foothold. At other times they descended into narrow valleys where they saw great numbers of wild animals of various kinds, some of which the Indians killed for food. After they reached the mountain district they loosed the hands of their prisoners, in order to enable them to climb more easily. Indeed in many places they had to scramble so carefully that it would have been impossible for any one to climb with his hands tied behind his back. But the Indians knew full well that they ran no risk of losing their prisoners; for if they had attempted to escape, dozens of their number were on the watch, before, behind, and on either side, ready to dart away in pursuit. Moreover, Barney had a feeling of horror at the bare idea of the poisoned arrows, that effectually prevented him from making the smallest attempt at escape. With a cutlass or a heavy stick he would have attacked the whole tribe single-handed, and have fought till his brains were knocked out; but when he thought of the small arrows that would pour upon him in hundreds if he made a dash for the woods, and the certain death that would follow the slightest scratch, he discarded all idea of rebellion.

One of the animals killed by the Indians at this time was a black jaguar—a magnificent animal, and very fierce. He was discovered crouching in a thicket backed by a precipice, from which he could only escape by charging through the ranks of his enemies. He did it nobly. With a roar that rebounded from the face of the high cliff and echoed through the valley like a peal of thunder, he sprang out and rushed at the savages in front, who scattered like chaff right and left. But at the same instant fifty blow-pipes sent their poisoned shafts into his body, and, after a few convulsive bounds, the splendid monarch of the American forests fell dead on the ground. The black jaguar is a somewhat rare animal, and is very seldom seen. This one was therefore hailed as a great prize, and the skin and claws were carefully preserved.

On the afternoon of the same day the party came to a broad stream, over which they, or some other of the numerous tribes in the country, had constructed a very simple and curious bridge. It was a single rope attached to an immense mass of rock on one side and to the stem of a large tree on the other. On this tight-rope was fastened a simple loop of cord, so constructed that it could encircle the waist of a man and at the same time traverse from one end of the tight-rope to the other. Barney put on a comical frown when he came to this and saw the leader of the party rest his weight in the loop, and, clinging with hands and legs to the long rope, work himself slowly across.

"Arrah! it's well for us, Martin, that we're used to goin' aloft," said he, " or that same bridge would try our narves a little."

"So it would, Barney. I've seldom seen a more

uncomfortable-looking contrivance. If we lost our hold we should first be dashed to pieces on the rocks, and then be drowned in the river."

Difficult though the passage seemed, however, it was soon accomplished by the active savages in safety. The only one of the party likely to be left behind was Grampus; whom his master, after much entreaty in dumb-show, was permitted to carry over by tying him firmly to his shoulders. Marmoset crossed over walking, like a tight-rope dancer, being quite *au fait* at such work. Soon after they came to another curious bridge over a ravine. It had been constructed by simply felling two tall trees on the edge of it in such a manner that they fell across. They were bound together with the supple vines that grew there in profusion. Nature had soon covered the whole over with climbing-plants and luxuriant verdure; and the bridge had become a broad and solid structure over which the whole party marched with perfect ease. Several such bridges were crossed, and also a few of the rope kind, during the journey.

After many weeks' constant travelling, the Indians came to a beautiful valley one evening just about sunset, and began to make the usual preparations for encamping. The spot they selected was a singular one. It was at the foot of a rocky gorge, up which might be seen trees and bushes mingled with jagged rocks and dark caverns, with a lofty sierra or mountain range in the background. In front was the beautiful valley which they had just crossed. On a huge rock there grew a tree of considerable size, the roots of which projected beyond the rock several yards, and then, bending downwards, struck into the ground. Creeping-plants had twined thickly among the roots, and thus formed a sort of lattice-work which enclosed a large space of ground. In this natural arbour the chiefs of the Indians took up their quarters and kindled their fire in the centre of it, while the main body of the party pitched their camp outside. The three prisoners were allotted a corner in the arbour; and, after having supped, they spread their ponchos on a pile of ferns, and found themselves very snug indeed.

"Martin," said Barney gravely, as he smoked his pipe and patted the head of his dog, " d'ye know I'm beginning to feel tired o' the company o' thim naked rascals, and I've been revolvin' in my mind what we should do to escape. Moreover, I've comed to a conclusion."

"And what's that?" inquired Martin.

"That it's unposs'ble to escape at all, and I don't know what to do."

"That's not a satisfactory conclusion, Barney. I, too, have been cogitating a good deal about these Indians, and it is my opinion that they have been on a war expedition, for I've noticed that several of them have been wounded; and, besides, I cannot fancy what else could take them so far from home."

"True, Martin, true. I wonder what they intind to do with us. They don't mean to kill us, anyhow, for if they did they would niver take the trouble to bring us here. Ochone! me heart's beginnin' to go down altogether, for we are miles and miles away from anywhere now, and I don't know the direction o' no place whatsumdiver."

"Never mind, Barney, cheer up," said Martin with a smile; "if they don't kill us, that's all we need care about. I'm sure we shall manage to escape somehow or other in the long-run."

While they thus conversed the old trader spread his poncho over himself and was soon sound asleep; while the Indians, after finishing supper, held an animated conversation. At times they seemed to be disputing, and spoke angrily and with violent gesticulations, glancing now and then at the corner where their prisoners lay.

"It's my belafe," whispered Barney, "that they're spakin' about us. I'm afeard they don't mean us any good. Och, but if I wance had my pistol and the ould cutlass. Well, well, it's of no manner o' use frettin'. Good-night, Martin, good-night!"

The Irishman knocked the ashes out of his pipe, turned his face to the wall, and, heaving a deep sigh, speedily forgot his cares in sleep. The Indians also lay down, the camp-fires died slowly out, and the deep breathing of the savages alone betokened the presence of man in that lone wilderness.

Barney's forebodings proved to be only too well founded, for next morning, instead of pursuing their way together, as usual, the savages divided their forces into two separate bands, placing the Irishman and the old trader in the midst of one, and Martin Rattler with the other.

"Surely they're niver goin' to part us, Martin," said Barney with a careworn expression on his honest countenance that indicated the anxious suspicions in his heart.

"I fear it much," replied Martin with a startled look, as he watched the proceedings of the Indians. "We must fight now, Barney, if we should die for it. We *must* not be separated."

Martin spoke with intense fervour, and gazed anxiously in the face of his friend. A dark frown had gathered there. The sudden prospect of being forcibly torn from his young companion, whom he regarded with almost a mother's tenderness, stirred his enthusiastic and fiery temperament to its centre, and he gazed wildly about, as if for some weapon. But the savages anticipated his intention. Ere he could grasp any offensive weapon two of their number leaped upon him, and at the same moment Martin's arms were pinioned in a powerful grasp.

"Och, ye murderin' blackguards!" cried Barney, hitting out right and left and knocking down a savage at each blow, "now or niver! come on, ye kangaroos!"

A general rush was made upon the Irishman, who was fairly overturned by the mass of men. Martin struggled fiercely to free himself, and would have succeeded had not two powerful Indians hastened to the help of the one who had first seized him. Despite his frantic efforts, he was dragged forcibly up the mountain gorge, the echoes of which rang with his cries as he shouted despairingly the name of his friend. Barney fought like a tiger, but he could make no impression on such numbers. Although at least a dozen Indians lay around him bleeding and stunned by the savage blows of his fists—a species of warfare which was entirely new to them—fresh savages crowded round. But they did not wish to kill him, and numerous though they were they found it no easy matter to secure so powerful a man; and when Martin turned a last despairing glance towards the camp, ere a turn in the path shut it out from view, the hammer-like fists of his comrade were still smashing down the naked creatures who danced like monkeys round him, and the warlike shouts of his stentorian voice reverberated among the cliffs and caverns of the mountain pass long after he was hid from view.

Thus Martin and Barney were separated in the wild regions near the Sierra dos Parecis of Brazil.

CHAPTER XX.

Martin reflects much, and forms a firm resolve—The Indian village.

WHEN the mind has been overwhelmed by some sudden and terrible calamity, it is long ere it again recovers its wonted elasticity. An aching void seems to exist in the heart, and a dead weight appears to press upon the brain, so that ordinary objects make but little impression, and the soul seems to turn inwards and brood drearily upon itself. The spirit of fun and frolic, that had filled Martin Rattler's heart ever since he landed in Brazil, was now so thoroughly and rudely crushed that he felt as if it were utterly impossible that he should ever smile again.

He had no conception of the strength of his affection for the rough, hearty sailor who had until now been the faithful and good-humoured companion of his wanderings. As Barney had himself said on a former occasion, his life up till this period had been a pleasant and exciting dream. But he was now rudely awakened to the terrible reality of his forlorn position; and the more he thought of it, the more hopeless and terrible it appeared to be.

He knew not in what part of Brazil he was; he was being hurried apparently deeper into these vast solitudes by savages who were certainly not friendly, and of whose language he knew not a word; and, worst of all, he was separated, perhaps for ever, from the friend on whom, all unconsciously to himself, he had so long leaned for support in all their difficulties and dangers. Even though he and Barney should succeed in escaping from the Indians, he felt—and his heart was overwhelmed at the thought—that in such a vast country there was not the shadow of a chance that they should find each other. Under the deep depression produced by these thoughts Martin wandered on wearily, as if in a dream, taking no interest in anything that occurred by the way. At length, after several days' fatiguing journey over mountains and plains, they arrived at the Indian village.

Here the warriors were received with the utmost joy by the wives and children whom they had left behind, and for a long time Martin was left almost entirely to do as he pleased. A few days before, his bonds had been removed, and once or twice he thought of attempting to escape; but whenever he wandered a little further than usual into the woods, he found that he was watched and followed by a tall and powerful savage, whose duty it evidently was to see that the prisoner did not escape. The fearful idea now entered Martin's mind that he was reserved for torture, and perhaps a lingering death; for he had read that many savage nations treated their prisoners in this cruel manner, for the gratification of the women who had lost relations in the war. But as no violence was offered to him in the meantime, and he had as much farina and fruit to eat as he could use, his mind gradually became relieved, and he endeavoured as much as possible to dismiss the terrible thought altogether.

The Indian village occupied a lovely situation at the base of a gentle hill or rising ground, the summit of which was clothed with luxuriant trees and shrubs. The huts were of various shapes and sizes, and very simple in construction. They were built upon the bare ground. Some were supported by four corner posts, twelve or fifteen feet high, and from thirty to forty feet long, the walls being made of thin laths connected with wicker-work and plastered with clay. The doors were made of palm-leaves, and the roofs were covered with the same material, or with maize straw. Other huts were made almost entirely of palm-leaves and were tent-shaped in form; and, while a few were enclosed by walls, the most of the square ones had one or more sides entirely open. In the large huts several families dwelt together, and each family had a hearth and a portion of the floor allotted to it. The smoke from their fires was allowed to find its way out by the doors and chinks in the roofs, as no chimneys were constructed for its egress.

The furniture of each hut was very simple. It consisted of a few earthen pots; baskets made of palm-leaves, which were filled with Spanish potatoes, maize, mandioca roots, and various kinds of wild fruits; one or two drinking vessels; the hollow trunk of a tree, used for pounding maize in; and several dishes which contained the colours used by the Indians in painting their naked bodies—a custom which was very prevalent amongst them. Besides these things, there were bows, arrows, spears, and blow-pipes in abundance; and hammocks hung from various posts, elevated about a foot from the ground. These hammocks were made of cotton cords, and served the purpose of tables, chairs, and beds.

The ground in the immediate neighbourhood of the village was laid out in patches, in which were cultivated mandioca roots, maize, and other plants useful for domestic purposes. In front of the village there was an extensive valley, through which a small river gurgled with a pleasant sound. It was hemmed in on all sides by wooded mountains, and was so beautifully diversified by scattered clusters of palms, and irregular patches of undulating grassy plains all covered with a rich profusion of tropical flowers and climbing-plants, that it seemed to Martin more like a magnificent garden than the uncultivated forest—only far more rich and lovely and picturesque than any artificial garden could possibly be. When the sun shone in full splendour on this valley—as it almost always did—it seemed as if the whole landscape were on the point of bursting into flames of red and blue, and green and gold; and when Martin sat under the shade of a tamarind tree and gazed long upon the enchanting scene, his memory often reverted to the Eden of which he used to read in the Bible at home, and he used to wonder if it were possible that the sun and flowers and trees *could* be more lovely in the time when Adam walked with God in Paradise.

Martin was young then, and he did not consider, although he afterwards came to know, that it was not the beauty of natural objects, but the presence and favour of God and the absence of sin, that rendered the Garden of Eden a paradise. But these thoughts always carried him back to dear old Aunt Dorothy and the sweet village of Ashford; and the Brazilian paradise was not unfrequently obliterated in tears while he gazed, and turned into a vale of weeping. Ay, he would have given that magnificent valley— had it been his own—ten times over, in exchange for one more glance at the loved faces and the green fields of home.

Soon after his arrival at the Indian village Martin was given to understand, by signs, that he was to reside with a particular family, and work every day in the maize and mandioca fields, besides doing a great deal of the drudgery of the hut; so that he now knew he was regarded as a slave by the tribe into whose hands he had fallen. It is impossible to express the bitterness of his feelings at this discovery, and for many weeks he went about his work scarcely knowing what he did, and caring little, when the hot sun beat on him so fiercely that he could hardly stand, whether he lived or died. At length, however, he made up his mind firmly to attempt his escape. He was sitting beneath the shade of his favourite resort, the tamarind tree, when he made this resolve. Longing thoughts of home had been strong upon him all that day, and desire for the companionship of

Barney had filled his heart to bursting; so that the sweet evening sunshine and the beautiful vale over which his eyes wandered, instead of affording him pleasure, seemed but to mock his misery. It was a lesson that all must learn sooner or later, and one we would do well to think upon before we learn it, that sunshine in the soul is not dependent on the sunshine of this world; and when once the clouds descend, the brightest beams of all that earth contains cannot pierce them. God alone can touch these dark clouds with the finger of love and mercy, and say again, as he said of old, " Let there be light."

A firm purpose, formed with heart and will, is cheering and invigorating to a depressed mind. No sooner did the firm determination to escape or die enter into Martin's heart, than he sprang from his seat, and, falling on his knees, prayed to God, in the name of our Redeemer, for help and guidance. He had not the least idea of how he was to effect his escape, or of what he intended to do. All he knew was that he had *made up his mind* to do so, *if God would help him.* And under the strength of that resolve he soon recovered much of his former cheerfulness of disposition, and did his work among the savages with a degree of energy that filled them with surprise and respect. From that day forth he never ceased to revolve in his mind every imaginable and unimaginable plan of escape, and to watch every event or circumstance, no matter how trifling, that seemed likely to aid him in his purpose.

Seeing that he was a very strong and active fellow, and that he had become remarkably expert in the use of the bow and the blow-pipe, the Indians now permitted Martin to accompany them frequently on their short hunting expeditions, so that he had many opportunities of seeing more of the wonderful animals and plants of the Brazilian forests, in the studying of which he experienced great delight. Moreover, in the course of a few months he began to acquire a smattering of the Indian language, and was not compelled to live in constant silence, as had been the case at first. But he carefully avoided the formation of any friendships with the youths of the tribe, although many of them seemed to desire it, considering that his doing so might in some way or other interfere with the execution of his great purpose. He was civil and kind to them all, however, though reserved; and, as time wore away, he enjoyed much more liberty than was the case at first. Still, however, he was watched by the tall savage, who was a surly, silent fellow, and would not be drawn into conversation. Indeed he did not walk with Martin, but followed him wherever he went, during his hours of leisure, at a distance of a few hundred yards, moving when his prisoner moved, and stopping when he halted, so that Martin at last began to regard him more as a shadow than a man.

CHAPTER XXI.

Savage feasts and ornaments—Martin grows desperate, and makes a bold attempt to escape.

HUNTING and feasting were the chief occupations of the men of the tribe with whom Martin sojourned. One day Martin was told that a great feast was to take place, and he was permitted to attend. Accordingly, a little before the appointed time he hastened to the large hut in and around which the festivities were to take place, in order to witness the preparations.

The first thing that struck him was that there seemed to be no preparations making for eating; and on inquiry he was told that they did not meet to eat, they met to drink and dance—those who were hungry might eat at home. The preparations for drinking were made on an extensive scale by the women, a number of whom stood round a large caldron, preparing its contents for use. These women wore very little clothing, and their bodies, besides being painted in a fantastic style, were also decorated with flowers and feathers. Martin could not help feeling that, however absurd the idea of painting the body was, it had at least the good effect of doing away to some extent with the idea of nakedness; for the curious patterns and devices gave to the Indians the appearance of being clothed in tights—and, at any rate, he argued mentally, paint was better than nothing. Some of the flowers were artificially constructed out of beetles' wings, shells, fish-scales, and feathers, and were exquisitely beautiful as well as gorgeous.

One of the younger women struck Martin as being ultra-fashionable in her paint. Her black shining hair hung like a cloak over her reddish-brown shoulders, and various strange drawings and figures ornamented her face and breast. On each cheek she had a circle, and over that two strokes. Under the nose were four red spots. From the corners of her mouth to the middle of each cheek were two parallel lines, and below these several upright stripes. On various parts of her back and shoulders were curiously entwined circles, and the form of a snake was depicted in vermilion down each arm. Unlike the others, she wore no ornament except a simple necklace of monkeys' teeth. This beauty was particularly active in manufacturing the intoxicating drink, which was prepared thus :—A quantity of maize was pounded in the hollow trunk of a tree, and put into an earthen pot, where it was boiled in a large quantity of water. Then the women took the coarsely-ground and boiled flour out of the water, chewed it in their mouths for a little, and put it into the pot again! By this means the decoction began to ferment and became intoxicating. It was a very disgusting method; yet it is practised by many Indian tribes in America, and, strange to say, also by some of the South Sea Islanders, who, of course, could not have learned it from these Indians.

When this beverage was ready, the chief, a tall, broad-shouldered man, whose painted costume and ornaments were most elaborate, stepped up to the pot and began a strange series of incantations, which he accompanied by rattling a small wooden instrument in his hand; staring all the time at the earthen pot, as if he half expected it to run away, and dancing slowly round it, as if to prevent such a catastrophe from taking place. The oftener the song was repeated the more solemn and earnest became the expression of his face and the tones of his voice. The rest of the Indians, who were assembled to the number of several hundreds, stood motionless round the pot, staring at him intently without speaking, and only now and then, when the voice and actions of the chief became much excited, they gave vent to a sympathetic howl.

After this had gone on for some time, the chief seized a drinking-cup, or *cuja*, which he gravely dipped into the pot and took a sip. Then the shaking of the rattle and the monotonous song began again. The chief next took a good pull at the cup and emptied it; after which he presented it to his companions, who helped themselves at pleasure; and the dance and monotonous music became more furious and noisy the longer the cup went round.

When the cup had circulated pretty freely among them, their dances and music became more lively, but they were by no means attractive. After he had watched them a short time, Martin left the festive scene with a feeling of pity for the poor savages, and as he thought upon their low and debased condition he recalled to mind the remark of his old friend the hermit—"They want the Bible in Brazil."

During his frequent rambles in the neighbourhood of the Indian village, Martin discovered many beautiful and retired spots, to which he was in the habit of going in the evenings after his daily labours were accomplished—accompanied, as usual, at a respectful distance, by his vigilant friend the tall savage. One of his favourite resting-places was at the foot of a banana tree which grew on the brow of a stupendous cliff about a mile distant from the hut in which he dwelt. From this spot he had a commanding view of the noble valley and the distant mountains. These mountains now seemed to the poor boy to be the ponderous gates of his beautiful prison, for he had been told by one of his Indian friends that on the other side of them were great campos and forests, beyond which dwelt many Portuguese, while still farther on was a great lake without shores, which was the end of the world. This, Martin was convinced, must be the Atlantic Ocean, for, upon inquiry, he found that many months of travel must be undergone ere it could be reached. Moreover, he knew that it could not be the Pacific, because the sun rose in that direction.

Sauntering away to his favourite cliff, one fine evening towards sunset, he seated himself beneath the banana tree and gazed longingly at the distant mountains, whose sharp summits glittered in the ruddy glow. He had long racked his brain in order to devise some method of escape, but hitherto without success. Wherever he went the "shadow" followed him, armed with the deadly blow-pipe; and he knew that even if he did succeed in eluding his vigilance and escaping into the woods, hundreds of savages would turn out and track him, with unerring certainty, to any hiding-place. Still the strength of his stern determination sustained him, and at each failure in his efforts to devise some means of effecting his purpose he threw off regret with a deep sigh, and returned to his labour with a firmer step, assured that he should eventually succeed.

As he sat there on the edge of the precipice he said, half aloud, "What prevents me from darting suddenly on that fellow and knocking him down?"

This was a question that might have been easily answered. No doubt he was physically capable of coping with the man, for he had now been upwards of a year in the wilderness, and was in his sixteenth year, besides being unusually tall and robust for his age. Indeed he looked more like a full-grown man than a stripling, for hard, incessant toil had developed his muscles and enlarged his frame, and his stirring life, combined latterly with anxiety, had stamped a few of the lines of manhood on his sunburnt countenance. But, although he could have easily overcome the Indian, he knew that he would be instantly missed, and from what he had seen of the powers of the savages in tracking wild animals to their dens in the mountains, he felt that he could not possibly elude them except by stratagem.

Perplexed and wearied with unavailing thought and anxiety, Martin pressed his hands to his forehead and gazed down the perpendicular cliff, which was elevated fully a hundred feet above the plain below. Suddenly he started, and clasped his hands upon his eyes, as if to shut out some terrible object from his sight. Then, creeping cautiously towards the edge of the cliff, he gazed down, while an expression of stern resolution settled upon his pale face.

And well might Martin's cheek blanch, for he had hit upon a plan of escape which, to be successful, required that he should twice turn a bold, unflinching face on death. The precipice, as before mentioned, was fully a hundred feet high, and quite perpendicular. At the foot of it there flowed a deep and pretty wide stream, which, just under the spot where Martin stood, collected in a deep black pool, where it rested for a moment ere it rushed on its rapid course down the valley. Over the cliff and into that pool Martin made up his mind to plunge, and so give the impression that he had fallen over and been drowned. The risk he ran in taking such a tremendous leap was very great indeed, but that was only half the danger he must encounter.

The river was one of a remarkable kind, of which there are one or two instances in South America.

It flowed down the valley between high rocks, and, a few hundred yards below the pool, it ran straight against the face of a precipice and there terminated to all appearance; but a gurgling vortex in the deep water at the base of the cliff, and the disappearance of everything that entered it, showed that the stream found a subterranean passage. There was no sign of its reappearance, however, in all the country round. In short, the river was lost in the bowels of the earth.

From the pool to the cliff where the river was engulfed the water ran like a mill-race, and there was no spot on either bank where any one could land, or even grasp with his hand, except one. It was a narrow, sharp rock that jutted out about two feet from the bank, quite close to the vortex of the whirlpool. This rock was Martin's only hope. To miss it would be certain destruction. But if he should gain a footing on it he knew that he could climb by a narrow fissure into a wild, cavernous spot, which it was exceedingly difficult to reach from any other point. A bend in the river concealed this rock and the vortex from the place whereon he stood, so that he hoped to be able to reach the point of escape before the savage could descend the slope and gain the summit of the cliff from whence it could be seen.

Of all this Martin was well aware, for he had been often at the place before, and knew every inch of the ground. His chief difficulty would be to leap over the precipice in such a manner as to cause the Indian to believe he had fallen over accidentally. If he could accomplish this, then he felt assured the savages would suppose he had been drowned, and so make no search for him at all. Fortunately the ground favoured this. About five feet below the edge of the precipice there was a projecting ledge of rock nearly four feet broad and covered with shrubs. Upon this it was necessary to allow himself to fall. The expedient was a desperate one, and he grew sick at heart as he glanced down the awful cliff, which seemed to him three times higher than it really was, as all heights do when seen from above.

Glancing round, he observed his savage guardian gazing contemplatively at the distant prospect. Martin's heart beat audibly as he rose and walked with an affectation of carelessness to the edge of the cliff. As he gazed down, a feeling of horror seized him; he gasped for breath, and almost fainted. Then the idea of perpetual slavery flashed across his mind, and the thought of freedom and home nerved him. He clinched his hands, staggered convulsively forward, and fell, with a loud and genuine shriek of terror, upon the shrubs that covered the rocky ledge. Instantly he arose, ground his teeth together, raised his eyes for one moment to heaven, and sprang into the air. For one instant he swept through empty space, the next he was deep down in the waters of the dark pool; and when the horrified Indian reached the edge of the precipice, he beheld his prisoner struggling on the surface for a moment, ere he was swept by the rapid stream round the point and out of view.

Bounding down the slope, the savage sped like a hunted antelope across the intervening space between the two cliffs, and quickly gained the brow of the lower precipice, which he reached just in time to see Martin Rattler's straw hat dance for a moment on the troubled waters of the vortex and disappear in the awful abyss. But Martin saw it too, from the cleft in the frowning rock.

On reaching the surface after his leap he dashed the water from his eyes and looked with intense earnestness in the direction of the projecting rock towards which he was hurried. Down he came upon it with such speed that he felt no power of man could resist. But there was a small eddy just below it, into which he was whirled as he stretched forth his hands and clutched the rock with the energy of despair. He was instantly torn away. But another small point projected two feet below it. This he seized. The water swung his feet to and fro as it gushed into the vortex, but the eddy saved him. In a moment his breast was on the rock, then his foot, and he sprang into the sheltering cleft just a moment before the Indian came in view of the scene of his supposed death.

Martin flung himself with his face to the ground, and thought rather than uttered a heartfelt thanksgiving for his deliverance. The savage carried the news of his death to his friends in the Indian village, and recounted with deep solemnity the particulars of his awful fate to crowds of wondering—in many cases sorrowing—listeners; and for many a day after that the poor savages were wont to visit the terrible cliff, and gaze with awe on the mysterious vortex that had swallowed up, as they believed, the fair-haired boy.

CHAPTER XXII.

The escape—Alone in the wilderness—Fight between a jaguar and an alligator—Martin encounters strange and terrible creatures.

FREEDOM can be fully appreciated only by those who have been for a long period deprived of liberty. It is impossible to comprehend the feelings of joy that welled up in Martin's bosom as he clambered up the rugged cliffs among which he had found shelter, and looked round upon the beautiful valley, now lying in the shadow of the mountain range behind which the sun had just set. He sat down on a rock, regardless of the wet condition of his clothes, and pondered long and earnestly over his position, which was still one of some danger; but a sensation of light-hearted recklessness made the prospect before him seem very bright. He soon made up his mind what to do. The weather was extremely warm, so that after wringing the water out of his linen clothes he experienced little discomfort; but he felt that there would not only be discomfort but no little danger in travelling in such a country without arms, covering, or provisions. He therefore determined on the bold expedient of revisiting the Indian village during the darkness of the night in order to procure what he required. He ran great risk of being retaken; but his necessity was urgent, and he was aware that several families were absent on a hunting expedition at that time whose huts were pretty certain to be unoccupied.

Accordingly, when two or three hours of the night had passed, he clambered with much difficulty down the precipitous rocks and reached the level plain, over which he quickly ran, and soon reached the outskirts of the village. The Indians were all asleep, and no sound disturbed the solemn stillness of the night. Going stealthily towards a hut, he peeped in at the open window, but could see and hear nothing. Just as he was about to enter, however, a long-drawn breath proved that it was occupied. He shrank hastily back into the deep shade of the bushes. In a few minutes he recovered from the agitation into which he had been thrown, and advanced cautiously towards another hut. This one seemed to be untenanted, so he opened the palm-leaf door gently and entered. No time was to be lost now. He found an empty sack or bag, into which he hastily threw as much farina as he could carry without inconvenience. Besides this, he appropriated a long knife, a small hatchet, a flint and steel to enable him to make a fire, and a stout bow, with a quiver full of arrows. It was so dark that it was with difficulty he found these things. But as he was on the point of leaving he observed a white object in a corner. This turned out to be a light hammock, which he seized eagerly, and, rolling it up into a small bundle, placed it in the sack. He also sought for, and fortunately found, an old straw hat, which he put on.

Martin had now obtained all that he required, and was about to quit the hut when he became suddenly rooted to the spot with horror on observing the dark countenance of an Indian gazing at him with distended eyeballs over the edge of a hammock. His eyes, unaccustomed to the darkness of the room, had not at first observed that an Indian was sleeping there. He now felt that he was lost. The savage evidently knew him. Dreadful thoughts flashed through his brain. He thought of the knife in his belt, and how easily he could despatch the Indian in a moment as he lay; but then the idea of imbruing his hands in human blood seemed so awful that he could not bring himself to do it.

As he looked steadily at the savage he observed

that his gaze was one of intense horror, and it suddenly occurred to him that the Indian supposed he was a ghost! Acting upon this supposition, Martin advanced his face slowly towards that of the Indian, put on a dark frown, and stood for a few seconds without uttering a word. The savage shrank back and shuddered from head to foot. Then, with a noiseless step, Martin retreated slowly backward towards the door and passed out like a spectre—never for a moment taking his eyes off those of the savage until he was lost in darkness. On gaining the forest he fled with a beating heart to his former retreat. But his fears were groundless, for the Indian firmly believed that Martin's spirit had visited his hut and carried away provisions for his journey to the land of spirits.

Without waiting to rest, Martin no sooner reached the scene of his adventurous leap than he fastened his bag firmly on his shoulders and struck across the valley in the direction of the blue mountains that hemmed it in. Four or five hours' hard walking brought him to their base, and long before the rising sun shone down upon his recent home he was over the hills and far away, trudging onward with a weary foot, but with a light heart, in what he believed to be the direction of the east coast of Brazil. He did not dare to rest until the rugged peaks of the mountain range were between him and the savages; but when he had left these far behind him, he halted about midday to breakfast and repose by the margin of a delightfully cool mountain stream.

"I'm safe now!" said Martin aloud, as he threw down his bundle beneath a spreading tree and commenced to prepare breakfast. "O my friend Barney, I wish that you were here to keep me company!" The solitary youth looked round as if he half expected to see the rough visage and hear the gladsome voice of his friend; but no voice replied to his, and the only living creature he saw was a large monkey, which peered inquisitively down at him from among the branches of a neighbouring bush. This reminded him that he had left his pet Marmoset in the Indian village, and a feeling of deep self-reproach filled his heart. In the haste and anxiety of his flight he had totally forgotten his little friend. But regret was now unavailing. Marmoset was lost to him for ever.

Having kindled a small fire, Martin kneaded a large quantity of farina in the hollow of a smooth stone, and baked a number of flat cakes, which were soon fired and spread out upon the ground. While thus engaged, a snake of about six feet long and as thick as a man's arm glided past him. Martin started convulsively, for he had never seen one of the kind before, and he knew that the bite of some of the snakes is deadly. Fortunately his axe was at hand. Grasping it quickly, he killed the reptile with a single blow. Two or three mandioca cakes, a few wild fruits, and a draught of water from the stream, formed the wanderer's simple breakfast. After it was finished, he slung his hammock between two trees, and jumping in, fell into a deep, untroubled slumber, in which he continued all that day and until daybreak the following morning.

After partaking of a hearty breakfast, Martin took up his bundle and resumed his travels. That day he descended into the level and wooded country that succeeded the mountain range, and that night he was obliged to encamp in a swampy place near a stagnant lake in which several alligators were swimming, and where the mosquitoes were so numerous that he found it absolutely impossible to sleep. At last, in despair, he sprang into the branches of the tree to which his hammock was slung and ascended to the top. Here, to his satisfaction, he found that there were scarcely any mosquitoes, while a cool breeze fanned his fevered brow, so he determined to spend the night in the tree.

By binding several branches together he formed a

rude sort of couch, on which he lay down comfortably, placing his knife and bow beside him, and using the hammock rolled up as a pillow. As the sun was setting, and while he leaned on his elbow looking down through the leaves with much interest at the alligators that gambolled in the reedy lake, his attention was attracted by a slight rustling in the bushes near the foot of the tree. Looking down, he perceived a large jaguar gliding through the underwood with cat-like stealth. Martin now observed that a huge alligator had crawled out of the lake, and was lying on the bank asleep a few yards from the margin. When the jaguar reached the edge of the bushes it paused, and then, with one tremendous spring, seized the alligator by the soft part beneath its tail. The huge monster struggled for a few seconds, endeavouring to reach the water, and then lay still, while the jaguar worried and tore at its tough hide with savage fury. Martin was much surprised at the passive conduct of the alligator. That it could not turn its stiff body so as to catch the jaguar in its jaws did not indeed surprise him, but he wondered very much to see the great reptile suffer pain so quietly. It seemed to be quite paralyzed. In a few minutes the jaguar retired a short distance. Then the alligator made a rush for the water; but the jaguar darted back and caught it again, and Martin now saw that the jaguar was actually playing with the alligator as a cat plays with a mouse before she kills it! During one of the cessations of the combat, if we may call it by that name, the alligator almost gained the water, and in the short struggle that ensued both animals rolled down the bank and fell into the lake. The tables were now turned. The jaguar made for the shore; but before it could reach it the alligator wheeled round, opened its tremendous jaws and caught its enemy by the middle. There was one loud splash in the water, as the alligator's powerful tail dashed it into foam, and one awful roar of agony, which was cut suddenly short and stifled as the monster dived to the bottom with its prey; then all was silent as the grave, and a few ripples on the surface were all that remained to tell of the battle that had been fought there.

Martin remained motionless on the tree top, brooding over the fight which he had just witnessed, until the deepening shadows warned him that it was time to seek repose. Turning on his side he laid his head on his pillow, while a soft breeze swayed the tree gently to and fro and rocked him sound asleep.

Thus, day after day, and week after week, did Martin Rattler wander alone through the great forests, sometimes pleasantly, and at other times with more or less discomfort; subsisting on game which he shot with his arrows, and on wild fruits. He met with many strange adventures by the way, which would fill numerous volumes were they to be written every one; but we must pass over many of these in silence, that we may recount those that were most interesting.

One evening, as he was walking through a very beautiful country, in which were numerous small lakes and streams, he was suddenly arrested by a crashing sound in the underwood, as if some large animal were coming towards him; and he had barely time to fit an arrow to his bow when the bushes in front of him were thrust aside, and the most hideous monster that he had ever seen appeared before his eyes. It was a tapir; but Martin had never heard of or seen such creatures before, although there are a good many in some parts of Brazil.

The tapir is a very large animal—about five or six feet long and three or four feet high. It is in appearance something between an elephant and a hog. Its nose is very long, and extends into a short proboscis; but there is no finger at the end of it like that of the elephant. Its colour is a deep brownish black, its tough hide is covered with a thin sprinkling of strong hairs, and its mane is thick and bristly. So thick is its hide that a bullet can scarcely penetrate it; and it can crush its way through thickets and bushes, however dense, without receiving a scratch. Although a very terrific animal to look at, it is fortunately of a very peaceable and timid disposition, so that it flees from danger, and is very quick in discovering the presence of an enemy. Sometimes it is attacked by the jaguar, which springs suddenly upon it and fastens its claws in its back; but the tapir's tough hide is not easily torn, and he gets rid of his enemy by bouncing into the tangled bushes and bursting through them, so that the jaguar is very soon *scraped* off his back! The tapir lives as much in the water as on the land, and delights to wallow like a pig in muddy pools. It is, in fact, very similar in many of its habits to the great hippopotamus of Africa, but is not quite so large. It feeds entirely on vegetables, buds, fruits, and the tender shoots of trees, and always at night. During the daytime it sleeps. The Indians of Brazil are fond of its flesh, and they hunt it with spears and poisoned arrows.

But Martin knew nothing of all this, and fully expected that the dreadful creature before him would attack and kill him; for when he observed its coarse tough-looking hide, and thought of the slender arrows with which he was armed, he felt that he had no chance, and there did not happen to be a tree near him at the time up which he could climb.

With the energy of despair he let fly an arrow with all his force, but the weak shaft glanced from the tapir's side without doing it the slightest damage. Then Martin turned to fly, but at the same moment the tapir did the same, to his great delight and surprise. It wheeled round with a snort, and went off crashing through the stout underwood as if it had been grass, leaving a broad track behind it.

On another occasion he met with a formidable-looking but comparatively harmless animal, called the great ant-eater. This remarkable creature is about six feet in length, with very short legs and very long strong claws, a short curly tail, and a sharp snout, out of which it thrusts a long narrow tongue. It can roll itself up like a hedgehog, and when in this position might be easily mistaken for a bundle of coarse hay. It lives chiefly if not entirely upon ants.

When Martin discovered the great ant-eater, it was about to begin its supper, so he watched it. The plain was covered with ant-hills, somewhat pillar-like in shape. At the foot of one of these the animal made an attack, tearing up earth and sticks with its enormously strong claws, until it made a large hole in the hard materials of which the hill was composed.

Into this hole it thrust its long tongue, and immediately the ants swarmed upon it. The creature let its tongue rest till it was completely covered over with thousands of ants, then it drew it into its mouth and engulfed them all!

As Martin had no reason in the world for attempting to shoot the great ant-eater, and as he was, moreover, by no means sure that he could kill it if he were to try, he passed on quietly and left this curious animal to finish its supper in peace.

CHAPTER XXIII.

Martin meets with friends, and visits the diamond mines.

ONE day, after Martin had spent many weeks in wandering alone through the forest, during the course of which he was sometimes tempted to despair of seeing the face of man again, he discovered a beaten track, at the sight of which his heart bounded with delight. It was a Saturday afternoon when he made this discovery, and he spent the Sabbath day in rest beside it. For Martin had more than once called to remembrance the words which good Aunt Dorothy used to hear him repeat out of the Bible—" Remember the Sabbath day, to keep it holy." He had many long, earnest, and serious meditations in that silent forest, such as a youth would be very unlikely to have in almost any other circumstances, except, perhaps, on a sick-bed; and among other things he had been led to consider, that if he made no difference between Saturday and Sunday, he must certainly be breaking that commandment. So he resolved thenceforth to rest on the Sabbath day; and he found much benefit, both to mind and body, from this arrangement. During this particular Sabbath he rested beside the beaten track, and often did he walk up and down it a short way, wondering where it would lead him to; and several times he prayed that he might be led by it to the habitations of civilized men.

Next day, after breakfast, he prepared to set out; but now he was much perplexed as to which way he ought to go, for the track did not run in the direction in which he had been travelling, but at right angles to that way. While he still hesitated, the sound of voices struck on his ear, and he almost fainted with excitement; for besides the hope that he might now meet with friends, there was also the fear that those approaching might be enemies, and the sudden sound of the human voice, which he had not heard for so long, tended to create conflicting and almost overwhelming feelings in his breast. Hiding quickly behind a tree, he awaited the passing of the cavalcade; for the sounds of horses' hoofs were now audible.

In a few minutes a string of laden mules approached, and then six horsemen appeared, whose bronzed olive complexions, straw-hats, and ponchos betokened them Brazilians. As they passed, Martin hailed them in an unsteady voice. They pulled up suddenly, and drew pistols from their holsters; but on seeing only a fair youth armed with a bow, they replaced their weapons, and with a look of surprise rode up and assailed him with a volley of unintelligible Portuguese.

"Do any of you speak English?" inquired Martin, advancing.

One of the horsemen replied, "Yees, I spok one leet. Ver' smoll. Where you be com?"

"I have escaped from the Indians who live in the mountains far away over yonder. I have been wandering now for many weeks in the forest; and I wish to get to the sea-coast, or to some town where I may get something to do, that I may be enabled to return home."

"Ho!" said the horseman gravely. "You com vid us. Ve go vid goods to de diamond mines. Git vork dere, yees. Put you body on dat hoss."

As the Brazilian spoke he pointed to a spare horse, which was led, along with several others, by a Negro. Thanking him for his politeness, Martin seized the horse by the mane and vaulted into the saddle, if the rude contrivance on its back might be so designated. The string of mules then moved on, and Martin rode with a light heart beside this obliging stranger, conversing with much animation.

In a very short time he learned, through the medium of his own bad Portuguese and the Brazilian's worse English, that he was not more than a day's ride from one of the diamond mines of that province of Brazil which is named Minas Geraes; that he was still many leagues distant from the sea; and that he would be sure to get work at the mines if he wished it, for the chief overseer, the Baron Fagoni, was an amiable man, and very fond of the English, but he could not speak their language at all, and required an interpreter. "And," said the Brazilian, with a look of great dignity, "I hab de honour for be de 'terpreter."

"Ah!" exclaimed Martin, "then I am in good fortune, for I shall have a friend at court."

The interpreter smiled slightly and bowed, after which they proceeded for some time in silence.

Next evening they arrived at the mines; and, after seeing to the comfort of his horse, and inquiring rather hastily as to the welfare of his family, the interpreter conducted Martin to the overseer's house, in order to introduce him.

The Baron Fagoni stood smoking in the doorway of his dwelling as they approached, and the first impression that Martin received of him was anything but agreeable.

He was a large, powerful man, with an enormous red beard and moustache, and a sombrero-like hat that concealed nearly the whole of his face. He seemed an irritable man, too, for he jerked his arms about and stamped in a violent manner as they drew near, and instead of waiting to receive them, he entered the house hastily and shut the door in their faces.

"The Baron would do well to take lessons in civility," said Martin, colouring as he turned to the interpreter.

"Ah, he be a leet pecoolair, sometime! Nev'r mind. Ve vill go to him."

So saying, the interpreter opened the door and entered the hall where the overseer was seated at a desk writing, as if in violent haste. Seeing that he did not mean to take notice of them, the interpreter spoke to him in Portuguese; but he was soon interrupted by a sharp reply, uttered in a harsh, grating voice, by the overseer, who did not look up or cease from his work.

Again the interpreter spoke as if in some surprise; but he was cut short by the overseer uttering, in a deep stern voice, the single word "Obey."

With a low bow the interpreter turned away, and taking Martin by the arm led him into an inner apartment, where, having securely fastened the window, he said to him, " De Baron say you be von blackguard tief; go 'bout contrie for steal diamonds. He make pris'ner ov you. Adios."

So saying, the interpreter made his bow and retired, locking the door behind him, and leaving Martin standing in the middle of the room, staring before him in speechless amazement.

CHAPTER XXIV.

The diamond mines—More and more astonishing!

IF Martin Rattler was amazed at the treatment he experienced at the hands of his new acquaintances on arriving, he had occasion to be very much more surprised at what occurred three hours after his incarceration.

It was getting dark when he was locked up, and for upwards of two hours he was left in total darkness. Moreover, he began to feel very hungry, having eaten nothing since mid-day. He was deeply engaged in devising plans for his escape when he was interrupted by the door being unlocked and a Negro slave entering with four magnificent candles, made of bees'-wax, which he placed upon the table. Then he returned to the door, where another slave handed him a tray containing dishes, knives and forks, and, in short, all the requisites for laying out a supper-table. Having spread a clean linen cloth on the board, he arranged covers for two, and going to the door placed his head to one side and regarded his arrangements with much complacency, and without paying the slightest attention to Martin, who pinched himself in order to make sure he was not dreaming.

In a few minutes the second Negro returned with an enormous tray, on which were dishes of all sizes, from under whose covers came the most savoury odours imaginable. Having placed these symmetrically on the board, both slaves retired and relocked the door without saying a word.

At last it began to dawn on Martin's imagination that the overseer must be an eccentric individual, who found pleasure in taking his visitors by surprise. But although this seemed a possible solution of the difficulty, he did not feel satisfied with it. He could with difficulty resist the temptation to attack the viands, however, and was beginning to think of doing this, regardless of all consequences, when the door again opened and the Baron Fagoni entered, relocked the door, put the key in his pocket, and standing before his prisoner with folded arms, gazed at him intently from beneath his sombrero.

Martin could not stand this. "Sir," said he, starting up, "if this is a joke, you have carried it far enough; and if you really detain me here a prisoner, every feeling of honour ought to deter you from adding insult to injury."

To this sternly-delivered speech the Baron made no reply, but springing suddenly upon Martin, he grasped him in his powerful arms, and crushed him to his broad chest till he almost broke every bone in his body!

"Och! cushla, bliss yer young face! sure it's yersilf, an' no mistake! Kape still, Martin, dear. Let me look at ye, darlint! Ah! then, isn't it my heart that's been broken for months an' months past about ye?"

Reader, it would be utterly in vain for me to attempt to describe either the words that flowed from the lips of Martin Rattler and Barney O'Flannagan on this happy occasion, or the feelings that filled their swelling hearts. The speechless amazement of Martin, the ejaculatory exclamations of the Baron Fagoni, the rapid questions and brief replies, are all totally indescribable. Suffice it to say, that for full quarter of an hour they exclaimed, shouted, and danced round each other, without coming to any satisfactory knowledge of how each had got to the same place, except that Barney at last discovered that Martin had travelled there by chance, and he had reached the mines by "intuition." Having settled this point, they sobered down a little.

"Now, Martin, darlint," cried the Irishman, throwing aside his hat for the first time, and displaying his well-known jolly visage, of which the forehead, eyes, and nose alone survived the general inundation of red hair, "ye'll be hungry, I've small doubt; so sit ye down, lad, to supper, and you'll tell me yer story as ye go along, and afther that I'll tell ye mine, while I smoke my pipe—the ould cutty, boy, that has comed through fire and wather, sound as a bell and blacker than iver!"

The Baron held up the well-known instrument of fumigation, as he spoke, in triumph.

Supper was superb. There were venison steaks, armadillo cutlets, tapir hash, iguana pie, and an immense variety of fruits and vegetables, that would have served a dozen men, besides cakes and splendid coffee.

"You live well here, Barney—I beg pardon, Baron Fagoni," said Martin, during a pause in their meal; "how in the world did you come by that name?"

Barney winked expressively. "Ah, boy, I wish I may niver have a worse. Ye see, when I first comed here, about four months ago, I found that the mine was owned by an Irish gintleman; an', like all the race, he's a trump. He took to me at wance when he hear'd my voice, and then he took more to me when he comed to know me character; and says he to me wan day, 'Barney,' says he, 'I'm gettin' tired o' this kind o' life now, and if ye'll agree to stop here as overseer, and sind me the proceeds o' the mine to Rio Janeiro, a great city on the sea-coast, an' the capital o' Brazil, I'll give ye a good share o' the profits. But,' says he, 'ye'll need to pretind ye're a Roosian, or a Pole, or somethin' o' that kind; for the fellows in thim parts are great rascals, and there's a few Englishmen among them who would soon find out that ye're only a Jack-tar before the mast, and would chate ye at no allowance. But if ye could spake no language under the sun but the gibberish pecooliar to the unbeknown provinces o' Siberia, ye could escape detection as far as yer voice is consarned; and by lettin' yer beard grow as long as possible, and dressin' yersilf properly, ye might pass and be as dignified as the great Mogul.'

"'Musha!' said I, 'but if I don't spake me own tongue I'll have to be dumb altogither.'

"'No fear,' says he; 'I'll tache ye enough Portuguese in a month or two to begin with, an' ye'll pick it up aisy after that.' And sure enough I began, tooth and nail, and, by hard workin', got on faster than I expected; for I can spake as much o' the lingo now as tides me over needcessities, and I understand most o' what's said to me. Anyhow, I ginerally see what they're drivin' at."

"So, then, you're actually in charge of the mine?" said Martin in surprise.

"Jist so, boy; but I'm tired of it already—it's by no means so pleasant as I expected it would be—so I'm thinkin' o' lavin' it, and takin' to the say again. I'm longin' dreadful to see the salt wather wance more."

"But what will the owner say, Barney? won't he have cause to complain of your breaking your engagement?"

"Niver a bit, boy. He tould me, before we parted, that if I wanted to quit I was to hand over the consarn to the interpreter, who is an honest fellow, I belave; so I'm jist goin' to pocket a di'mond or two, and ask lave to take them home wid me. I'll be off in a week, if all goes well. An' now, Martin, fill yer glass—ye'll find the wine is not bad after wan or two glasses—an' I'll tell ye about my adventures since I saw ye last."

"But you have not explained about your name," said Martin.

"Och! the fact is, that when I comed here I fortunately fell in with the owner first, and we spoke almost intirely in Irish, so nobody understood where I comed from; and the interpreter hear'd the master call me by my name, so he wint off and said to the people that a great Barono Flanagoni had come, and was up at the house wid the master. But we corrected him afterwards, and gave him to understand that I was the Baron Fagoni. I had some trouble with the people at first, after the owner left; but I pounded wan or two o' the biggest o' them to sich a extint that their own friends hardly knew them, an' iver since they've been mighty civil."

Having carefully filled the black pipe, and involved himself in his own favourite atmosphere, the Baron Fagoni then proceeded to relate his adventures, and dilated upon them to such an extent that five or six pipes were filled and finished ere the story came to a close. Martin also related his adventures, to which his companion listened with such breathless attention and earnestness that his pipe was constantly going out, and the two friends did not retire to rest till near daybreak.

The substance of the Baron's narrative was as follows :—

At the time that he had been so suddenly separated from his friend, Barney had overcome many of his opponents, but at length he was overpowered by numbers, and his arms were firmly bound; after which he was roughly driven before them through the woods for several days, and was at length taken to their village among the mountains. Here he remained a close prisoner for three weeks, shut up in a small hut, and bound by a strong rope to a post. Food was taken to him by an old Indian woman, who paid no attention at first to what he said to her, for the good reason that she did not understand a word of English. The persuasive eloquence of her prisoner's tones, however, or perhaps his brogue, seemed in the course of a few days to have made an impression on her; for she condescended to smile at the unintelligible compliments which Barney lavished upon her in the hope of securing her good-will.

During all this time the Irishman's heart was torn with conflicting feelings; and although, from the mere force of habit, he could jest with the old woman when she paid her daily visits, there was no feeling of fun in his bosom, but, on the contrary, a deep and overwhelming sorrow, which showed itself very evidently on his expressive face. He groaned aloud when he thought of Martin, whom he never expected again to see; and he dreaded every hour the approach of his savage captors, who, he fully expected, retained him in order to put him to death.

One day, while he was sitting in a very disconsolate mood, the Indian woman entered with his usual dinner—a plate of thick soup and a coarse cake. Barney smiled upon her as usual, and then, letting his eyes fall on the ground, sighed deeply, for his heart was heavier than usual that day. As the woman was about to go, he looked earnestly and gravely in her face, and putting his large hand gently on her head, patted her gray hairs. This tender action seemed to affect the old woman more than usual. She laid her hand on Barney's arm, and looked as if she wished to speak. Then turning suddenly from him, she drew a small knife from her girdle and dropped it on the ground, as if accidentally, while she left the hut and refastened the door. Barney's heart leaped. He seized the knife and concealed it hastily in his bosom, and then ate his dinner with more than ordinary zest, for now he possessed the means of cutting the strong rope that bound him.

He waited with much impatience until night closed over the Indian village; and then cutting his bonds, he tore down the rude and rather feeble fastenings of the door. In another instant he was dashing along at full speed through the forest, without hat or coat, and with the knife clutched in his right hand! Presently he heard cries behind him, and redoubled his speed, for now he knew that the savages had discovered his escape and were in pursuit. But, although a good runner, Barney was no match for the lithe and naked Indians. They rapidly gained on him, and he was about to turn at bay and fight for his life, when he observed water gleaming through the foliage on his left. Dashing down a glade, he came to the edge of a broad river with a rapid current. Into this he sprang recklessly, intending to swim with the stream; but ere he lost his footing he heard the low, deep thunder of a cataract a short distance below! Drawing back in terror, he regained the bank, and waded up a considerable distance in the shallow water, so as to leave no trace of his footsteps. Then he leaped upon a rock, and catching hold of the lower branches of a large tree, drew himself up among the dense foliage, just as the yelling savages rushed with wild tumult to the water's edge. Here they paused, as if baffled. They spoke in rapid, vehement tones for a few seconds, and then one party hastened down the banks of the stream towards the fall, while another band searched the banks above.

Barney's heart fell as he sat panting in the tree, for he knew that they would soon discover him. But he soon resolved on a bold expedient. Slipping down from the tree, he ran deliberately back towards the village, and, as he drew near, he followed the regular beaten track that led towards it. On the way he encountered one or two savages hastening after the pursuing party; but he leaped lightly into the bushes, and lay still till they were past. Then he ran on, skirted round the village, and pushed into the woods in an entirely opposite direction from the one in which he had first set out. Keeping by one of the numerous tracks that radiated from the village into the forest, he held on at top speed, until his progress was suddenly arrested by a stream about twenty yards broad. It was very deep, and he was about to plunge in, in order to swim across, when he observed a small montaria or canoe lying on the bank. This he launched quickly, and observing that the river took a bend a little farther down, and appeared to proceed in the direction he wished to pursue—namely, away from the Indian village—he paddled down the rapid stream as fast as he could. The current was very strong, so that his little bark flew down it like an arrow, and on more than one occasion narrowly missed being dashed to pieces on the rocks which here and there rose above the stream.

In about two hours Barney came to a place where the stream took another bend to the left, and soon after the canoe swept out upon the broad river into which he had at first so nearly plunged. He was a long way below the fall now, for its sound was inaudible; but it was no time to abate his exertions. The Indians might be still in pursuit; so he continued to paddle all that night, and did not take rest until daybreak. Then he slept for two hours, ate a few wild fruits, and continued his journey.

In the course of the next day, to his great joy, he overtook a trading-canoe, which had been up another tributary of this river, and was descending with part of a cargo of india-rubber shoes. None of the men, of whom there were four, could speak English; but they easily saw from the Irishman's condition that he had escaped from enemies and was in distress, so they took him on board, and were glad to avail themselves of his services, for, as we have before mentioned, men are not easily procured for voyaging in those parts of Brazil. Three weeks after this they arrived at a small town, where the natives were busily engaged in the manufacture of shoes, bottles, and other articles of india-rubber, and here Barney found employment for a short time.

The seringa, or india-rubber tree, grows plentifully in some parts of Brazil, and many hundreds of the inhabitants are employed in the manufacture of shoes. The india-rubber is the juice of the tree, and flows from it when an incision is made. This juice is poured into moulds and left to harden. It is of a yellowish colour naturally, and is blackened in the course of preparation. Barney did not stay long here. Shoemaking, he declared, was not his calling by any means; so he seized the first opportunity he had of joining a party of traders going into the interior, in the direction of the diamond districts. The journey was long and varied—sometimes by canoe and sometimes on the backs of mules and horses—and many extraordinary adventures did he go through ere he reached the diamond mines; and when at length he did so, great was his disappointment. Instead of the glittering caves which his vivid imagination had pictured, he found that there were no caves at all; that the diamonds were found by washing in the muddy soil; and, worst of all, that when found they were dim and unpolished, so that they seemed no better than any other stone. However, he resolved to continue there for a short time, in order to make a little money; but now that Martin had arrived, he thought that they could not do better than make their way to the coast as fast as possible, and go to sea.

"The only thing I have to regret," he said, at the conclusion of his narrative, "is that I left Grampus behind me. But arrah! I came off from the savages in such a hurry that I had no time at all to tell him I was goin'!"

Having sat till daybreak, the two friends went to bed to dream of each other and of home.

Next morning Barney took Martin to visit the diamond mines. On the way they passed a band of Negro slaves who encircled a large fire, the weather being very cold. It was at that time about the end of July, which is one of the coldest months in the year. In this part of Brazil summer and winter are reversed—the coldest months being May, June, and July; the hottest, November, December, January, and February.

Minas Geraes, the diamond district, is one of the richest provinces of Brazil. The inhabitants are almost entirely occupied in mining or in supplying the miners with the necessaries of life. Diggers and shopkeepers are the two principal classes, and of these the latter are best off; for their trade is steady and lucrative, while the success of the miners is very uncertain. Frequently a large sum of money and much time are expended in mining without any adequate result; but the merchants always find a ready sale for their merchandise, and, as they take diamonds and gold-dust in exchange, they generally realize large profits, and soon become rich. The poor miner is like the gambler. He digs on in hope, sometimes finding barely enough to supply his wants, at other times making a fortune suddenly, but never giving up in despair, because he knows that at every handful of earth he turns up he may perhaps find a diamond worth hundreds or, it may be, thousands of pounds.

Cidade Diamantina—the City of Diamonds—is the capital of the province. It is a large city, with many fine churches and buildings; and the whole population, consisting of more than six thousand souls, are engaged, directly or indirectly, in mining. Every one who owns a few slaves employs them in washing the earth for gold and diamonds.

The mine of which Barney had so unexpectedly become overseer was a small one, in a remote part of the district, situated among the mountains, and far distant from the City of Diamonds. There were only a few huts, rudely built and roofed with palm-leaves, besides a larger building, or cottage, in which the Baron Fagoni resided.

" 'Tis a strange life they lead here," said Barney, as he led Martin down a gorge of the mountains towards a small spot of level ground on which the slaves were at work—" a strange life, and by no means a pleasant wan, for the feedin' is none o' the best and the work very sevare."

" Why, Barney, if I may judge from last night's supper, the feeding seems to be excellent."

"Thrue, boy, the Baron Fagoni feeds well, bekase he's the cock o' the roost; but the poor Naygurs are not overly well fed, and the craturs are up to their knees in wather all day, washing di'monds; so they suffer much from rheumatiz and colds. Och, but it's murther intirely, an' I've more than wance felt inclined to fill their pockets with di'monds and set them all free! Jist look, now; there they are, hard at it."

As he spoke they arrived at the mine. The ground in the vicinity was all cut up and dug out to a considerable depth, and a dozen Negroes were standing under a shed washing the earth, while others were engaged in the holes excavating the material. While Martin watched them his friend explained the process.

The different kinds of soil through which it is necessary to cut before reaching the diamond deposit are, first, about twenty feet of reddish sandy soil; then about eight feet of a tough yellowish clay; beneath this lies a layer of coarse reddish sand, below which is the peculiar soil in which diamonds are found. It is called by the miners the *cascalho*, and consists of loose gravel, the pebbles of which are rounded and polished, having at some previous era been subject to the action of running water. The bed varies in thickness from one to four feet, and the pebbles are of various kinds, but when there are many of a species called *esmerilo preto*, the cascalho is considered to be rich in diamonds.

Taking Martin round to the back of the shed, Barney showed him a row of troughs, about three feet square, close to the edge of a pond of water. These troughs are called *bacos*. In front of each stood a Negro slave up to the knees in water. Each had a wooden plate, with which he dashed water upon the rough cascalho as it was thrown into the trough by another slave. By this means, and by stirring it with a hoe, the earth and sand are washed away. Two overseers were closely watching the process, for it is during this part of the operation that the largest diamonds are found. These overseers were seated on elevated seats, each being armed with a long leathern whip, to keep a sharp look out, for the slaves are expert thieves.

After the cascalho had been thus purified it was carefully removed to the shed to be finally washed.

Here seven slaves were seated on the side of a small canal, about four feet broad, with their legs in the water nearly up to their knees. This canal is called the *lavadeira*. Each man had a small wooden platter, into which another slave, who stood behind him, put a shovelful of purified cascalho. The *bateia*, or platter, was then filled with water and washed with the utmost care several times, being closely examined after each washing, and the diamonds picked out. Sometimes many platefuls were examined but nothing found; at other times several diamonds were found in one plate. While Martin was looking on with much curiosity and interest, one of the slaves uttered an exclamation and held up a minute stone between his finger and thumb.

"Ah! good luck to ye, lad!" said Barney, advancing and taking the diamond which had been discovered. "See here, Martin; there's the thing, lad, that sparkles on the brow o' beauty, and gives the Naygurs rheumatiz—"

"Not to mention their usefulness in providing the great Baron Fagoni with a livelihood," added Martin, with a smile.

Barney laughed, and going up to the place where the two overseers were seated, dropped the precious gem into a plate of water placed between them for the purpose of receiving the diamonds as they were found.

"They git fifteen or twinty a day sometimes," said Barney, as they retraced their steps to the cottage; "and I've hear'd o' them getting stones worth many thousands o' pounds; but the biggest they iver found since I comed here was not worth more than four hundred."

"And what do you do with them, Barney, when they are found?" inquired Martin.

"Sind them to Rio Janeiro, lad, where my employer sells them. I don't know how much he makes a year by it, but the thing must pay, for he's very liberal with his cash, and niver forgits to pay wages. There's always a lot o' gould-dust found in the bottom o' the bateia after each washing, and that is carefully collected and sold. But, arrah! I wouldn't give wan snifter o' the say-breezes for all the di'monds in Brazil!"

As Barney said this he entered his cottage and flung down his hat with the air of a man who was resolved to stand it no longer.

"But why don't you wash on your own account?" cried Martin. "What say you—shall we begin together? We may make our fortune the first week, perhaps!"

Barney shook his head. "No, no, boy; I've no faith in my luck with the di'monds or gould. Nevertheless I have hear'd o' men makin' an awful heap o' money that way, partiklarly wan man that made his fortin with wan stone."

"Who was that lucky dog?" asked Martin.

"Well, ye see, it happened this way. There's a custom hereaway that slaves are allowed to work on Sundays and holidays on their own account; but when the mines was a government consarn this was not allowed, and the slaves were the most awful thieves livin', and often made off with some o' the largest di'monds. Well, there was a man named Juiz de Paz, who owned a small shop, and used to go down now and then to Rio de Janeiro to buy goods. Wan evenin' he returned from wan o' his long journeys, and, bein' rather tired, wint to bed. He was jist goin' off into a comfortable doze when there came a terrible bumpin' at the door.

"'Hallo!' cried Juiz, growlin' angrily in the Portugee tongue; 'what d'ye want?'

"There was no answer but another bumpin' at the door. So up he jumps, and, takin' down a big blunderbuss that hung over his bed, opened the door, an' seized a Naygur be the hair o' the head!

"'O massa! O massa! let him go! Got di'mond for to sell!'

"On hearin' this, Juiz let go, and found that the slave had come to offer for sale a large di'mond, which weighed about two pennyweights and a third.

"'What d'ye ask for it?' said Juiz, with sparklin' eyes.

"'Six hundred mil-reis,' answered the Naygur.

"This was about equal to one hundred and eighty pounds stirling. Without more words about it, he paid down the money, and the slave went away. Juiz lost his sleep that night. He went and tould the neighbours he had forgot a piece of important business in Rio and must go back at wance. So back he went, and stayed some time in the city, tryin' to git his di'mond safely sold; for it was sich a big wan that he feared the government fellows might hear o't, in which case he would have got tin years' transportation to Angola on the coast of Africa. At last, however, he got rid of it for twenty thousand mil-reis, which is about six thousand pounds. It was all paid to him in hard dollars, and he nearly went out o' his wits for joy. But he was brought down a peg nixt day, when he found that the same di'mond was sold for nearly twice as much as he had got for it. Howiver, he had made a pretty considerable fortin; an' he's now the richest di'mond and gould merchant in the district."

"A lucky fellow certainly," said Martin. "But I must say I have no taste for such chance work; so I'm quite ready to start for the sea-coast whenever it suits the Baron Fagoni's convenience."

While they were speaking they were attracted by

voices outside the cottage, which sounded as if in altercation. In another minute the door burst open, and a man entered hurriedly, followed by the interpreter.

"Your overseer is impertinent!" exclaimed the man, who was a tall swarthy Brazilian. "I wish to buy a horse or a good mule, and he won't let me have one. I am not a beggar; I offer to pay."

The man spoke in Portuguese, and Barney replied in the same language,—

"You can have a horse *if you pay for it.*"

The Brazilian replied by throwing a heavy bag of dollars on the table.

"All right," said Barney, turning to his interpreter and conversing with him in an under-tone. "Give him what he requires." So saying he bowed the Brazilian out of the room, and returned to the enjoyment of his black pipe, which had been interrupted by the incident.

"That man seems in a hurry," said Martin.

"So he is. My interpreter tells me that he is quite like one o' the blackguards that sometimes go about the mines doin' mischief, and he's in hot haste to be away. I shouldn't wonder if the spalpeen has been stealin' gould or di'monds and wants to escape. But of course I've nothin' to do with that, unless I was sure of it; and I've a horse or two to sell, and he has money to pay for it, so he's welcome. He says he is makin' straight for the say-coast; and with your lave, Martin, my boy, you and I will be doin' that same in a week after this, and say good-bye to the di'mond mines."

CHAPTER XXV.

New scenes and pleasant travelling.

A NEW and agreeable sensation is a pleasant thing. It was on as bright an evening as ever shone upon Brazil, and in as fair a scene as one could wish to behold, that Martin Rattler and his friend Barney experienced a new sensation. On the wide campos, on the flower-bedecked and grassy plains, they each bestrode a fiery charger; and in the exultation of health and strength and liberty, they swept over the greensward of the undulating campos as light as the soft wind that fanned their bronzed cheeks, as gay in heart as the buzzing insects that hovered above the brilliant flowers.

"Oh, this is best of all!" shouted Martin, turning his sparkling eyes to Barney, as he reined up his steed after a gallop that caused its nostrils to expand and its eyes to dilate. "There's nothing like it! A fiery charger that can't and *won't* tire, and a glorious sweep of plain like that! Huzza! whoop!" And loosening the rein of his willing horse, away he went again in a wild headlong career.

"Och, boy, pull up, or ye'll kill the baste!" cried Barney, who thundered along at Martin's side enjoying to the full the spring of his powerful horse; for Barney had spent the last farthing of his salary on the two best steeds the country could produce, being determined, as he said, to make the last overland voyage on clipper-built animals which, he wisely concluded, would fetch a good price at the end of the journey. "Pull up! d'ye hear? They can't stand goin' at that pace. Back yer topsails, ye young rascal, or I'll board ye in a jiffy."

"How can I pull up with *that* before me?" cried Martin, pointing to a wide ditch or gully that lay in front of them. "I must go over that first."

"Go over that!" cried Barney, endeavouring to rein in his horse, and looking with an anxious expression at the chasm. "It's all very well for you to talk o' goin' over, ye feather, but fifteen stun— Ah, then, *won't* ye stop? Bad luck to him, he's got the bit in his teeth! Oh then, ye ugly baste, go, and my blessin' go with ye!"

The leap was inevitable. Martin went over like a deer. Barney shut his eyes, seized the pommel of the saddle, and went at it like a thunderbolt. In the excitement of the moment he shouted in a stentorian voice, "Clap on all sail! d'ye hear? Stun-sails and sky-scrapers! Kape her steady! Hooray!"

It was well for Barney that he had seized the saddle. Even as it was he received a tremendous blow from the horse's head as it took the leap and was thrown back on its haunches when it cleared the ditch, which it did nobly.

"Hallo, old boy! not hurt, I hope," said Martin, suppressing his laughter as his comrade scrambled on to the saddle. "You travel about on the back of your horse at full gallop like a circus rider."

"Whist, darlint, I do belave he has damaged my faygur-head. What a nose I've got! Sure I can see it mesilf without squintin'."

"So you have, Barney. It's a little swelled, but never mind. We must all learn by experience, you know. So come along."

"Hould on, ye spalpeen, till I git my wind!"

But Martin was off again at full speed, and Barney's horse, scorning to be left behind, took the bit again in its teeth and went—as he himself expressed it— "screamin' before the wind." A new sensation is not always and necessarily an agreeable thing. Martin and Barney found it so on the evening of that same day, as they reclined (they could not sit) by the side of their fire on the campo under the shelter of one of the small trees which grew here and there at wide intervals on the plain. They had left the diamond mine early that morning, and their first day on horseback proved to them that there are shadows as well as lights in eq𝚞estrian life. Their only baggage was a single change of apparel and a small bag of diamonds—the latter being the product of the mine during the Baron Fagoni's reign, and which that worthy was conveying faithfully to his employer. During the first part of the day they had ridden through a hilly and wooded country, and towards evening they emerged upon one of the smaller campos which occur here and there in the district.

"Martin," said Barney, as he lay smoking his pipe, "'tis a pity that there's no pleasure in this world without *something* cross-grained into it. My own feelin's is as if I had been lately passed through a stamping machine."

"Wrong, Barney, as usual," said Martin, who was busily engaged concluding supper with an orange. "If we had pleasures without discomforts we wouldn't half enjoy them. We need lights and shadows in life—what are you grinning at, Barney?"

"Oh, nothin'! only ye're a re-markable philosopher, when ye're in the vein."

"'Tis always in vain to talk philosophy to you, Barney, so good night t'ye. Oh, dear me, I wish I could sit down! but there's no alternative—either bolt upright or quite flat."

In quarter of an hour they both forgot pleasures and sorrows alike in sleep. Next day the sun rose on the edge of the campo as it does out of the ocean, streaming across its grassy billows, and tipping the ridges as with ruddy gold. At first Martin and Barney did not enjoy the lovely scene, for they felt stiff and sore; but after half-an-hour's ride they began to recover, and when the sun rose in all its glory on the wide plain, the feelings of joyous, bounding freedom that such scenes always engender obtained the mastery, and they coursed along in silent delight.

The campo was hard, composed chiefly of a stiff red clay soil, and covered with short grass in most places; but here and there were rank bushes of long hairy grasses, around and amongst which grew a multitude of the most exquisitely beautiful flowerets and plants of elegant forms. Wherever these flowers flourished very luxuriantly, there were single trees of stunted growth and thick bark, which seldom rose above fifteen or twenty feet. Besides these there were rich flowering myrtles, and here and there a grotesque cactus or two.

Under one of these trees they reined up after a ride of two hours, and picketing their horses, prepared breakfast. It was soon despatched, and then remounting, away they went once more over the beautiful plains.

About mid-day, as they were hasting towards the shelter of a grove which appeared opportunely on the horizon, Barney said suddenly,—

"Martin, lad, we're lost! We're out of our course, for sartin."

"I've been thinking that for some time, Barney," replied Martin; "but you have your compass, and we can surely make the coast by dead reckoning—eh?"

"True, lad, we can; but it'll cost us a dale o' tackin' to make up for leeway. Ah, good luck to ye! here's a friend 'll help us."

As he spoke a herd of wild cattle dashed out of the grove and scampered over the plain, followed by a herdsman on horseback. Seeing that he was in eager pursuit of an animal which he wished to lasso, they followed him quietly and watched his movements. Whirling the noose round his head, he threw it adroitly in such a manner that the bull put one of its legs within the coil. Then he reined up suddenly, and the animal was thrown on its back. At the same moment the lasso broke, and the bull recovered its feet and continued its wild flight.

"Good-day, friend," said Barney, galloping towards the disappointed herdsman and addressing him in Portuguese, "could you show us the road to Rio? We've lost it entirely."

The man pointed sulkily in the direction in which they were going, and, having mended his lasso, he wheeled about and galloped after the herd of cattle.

"Bad luck to yer manners!" said Barney, as he gazed after him. "But what can ye expect from the poor cratur? He niver larned better. Come along, Martin; we'll rest here a while."

They were soon under the shelter of the trees, and having fastened their horses to one of them, they proceeded to search for water. While thus employed, Barney shouted to his companion, "Come here, lad; look here."

There was something in the tone of the Irishman's voice that startled Martin, and he sprang hastily towards him. Barney was standing with his arms crossed upon his chest and his head bowed forward, as he gazed with a solemn expression on the figure of a man at his feet.

"Is he ill?" inquired Martin, stooping and lifting his hand. Starting back as he dropped it, he exclaimed, "Dead!"

"Ay, boy, he has gone to his last account. Look

at him again, Martin. It was he who came to the mine a week ago to buy a horse, and now—" Barney sighed as he stooped and turned the body over in order to ascertain whether he had been murdered, but there were no marks of violence to be seen. There was bread, too, in his wallet; so they could come to no other conclusion than that the unhappy man had been seized with fatal illness in the lonesome wood and died there.

As they searched his clothes they found a small leathern bag, which, to their amazement, was filled with gold-dust, and in the midst of the gold was another smaller bag containing several small diamonds.

"Ha!" exclaimed Martin, "that explains his hurry. No doubt he had made off with these, and was anxious to avoid pursuit."

"No doubt of it," said Barney. "Well, thief or no thief, we must give the poor cratur dacent burial. There's not a scrap o' paper to tell who he is or where he came from—a sure sign that he wasn't what he should ha' been. Ah, Martin, what will we not do for the sake o' money? and, after all, we can't keep it long. May the Almighty niver let you or me set our hearts on it!"

They dug a shallow grave with their hands in a sandy spot where the soil was loose, in which they deposited the body of the unfortunate man, and then remounting their horses, rode away and left him in his lonely resting-place.

For many days did Martin and Barney travel through the land on horseback, now galloping over open campos, anon threading their way through the forest, and sometimes toiling slowly up the mountain sides. The aspect of the country varied continually as they advanced, and the feelings of excessive hilarity with which they commenced the journey began to subside as they became accustomed to it.

One evening they were toiling slowly up a steep range of hills which had been the prospect in front of them the whole of that day. As they neared the summit of the range Martin halted at a stream to drink, and Barney advanced alone. Suddenly Martin was startled by a loud cry, and looking up he saw Barney on his knees with his hands clasped before him. Rushing up the hill, Martin found his comrade with his face flushed and the tears coursing down his cheeks as he stared before him.

"Look at it, Martin, dear!" he cried, starting up and flinging his cap in the air, and shouting like a madman. "The say! my own native illiment! the beautiful ocean! Och, darlint, my blessin' on ye! Little did I think to see you more—hooray!"

Barney sang and danced till he sank down on the grass exhausted; and, to say truth, Martin felt much difficulty in restraining himself from doing likewise, for before him was spread out the bright ocean, gleaming in the light of the sinking sun, and calm and placid as a mirror. It was indeed a glorious sight to these two sailors, who had not seen the sea for nearly two years. It was like coming suddenly face to face, after a long absence, with an old and much-loved friend.

Although visible, the sea, however, was still a long way off from the Serra dos Orgaos, on which they stood. But their steeds were good, and it was not long ere they were both rolling like dolphins in the beautiful bay of Rio de Janeiro.

Here Barney delivered up the gold and diamonds to his employer, who paid him liberally for his services, and entertained them both hospitably while they remained in the city. The bag of gold and diamonds which had been found on the body of the dead man they appropriated, as it was absolutely impossible to discover the rightful owner. Barney's friend bought it of them at full price, and when they embarked, soon after, on board a homeward-bound ship, each had four hundred pounds in his pocket!

As they sailed out of the noble harbour, Martin

sat on the poop gazing at the receding shore while thick-coming memories crowded on his brain.

His imagination flew back to the day when he first landed on the coast and escaped with his friend Barney from the pirates—to the hermit's cottage in the lonely valley, where he first made acquaintance with monkeys, iguanas, jaguars, armadillos, and all the wonderful, beautiful, and curious birds, beasts, and reptiles, plants, trees, and flowers, that live and flourish in that romantic country. Once more, in fancy, he was sailing up the mighty Amazon, shooting alligators on its banks, spearing fish in its waters, paddling through its curious Gapo, and swinging in his hammock under its luxuriant forests. Once again he was a prisoner among the wild Indians, and he started convulsively as he thought of the terrible leap over the precipice into the stream that flowed into the heart of the earth. Then he wandered in the lonely forest. Suddenly the diamond mines were before him, and Barney's jovial voice rang in his ears, and he replied to it with energy, for now he was bounding on a fiery steed over the grassy campos. With a deep sigh he awoke from his reverie to find himself surrounded by the great wide sea.

CHAPTER XXVI.

The return.

ARTHUR JOLLYBOY, Esquire, of the Old Hulk, sat on the top of a tall three-legged stool in his own snug little office in the sea-port town of Bilton, with his legs swinging to and fro; his socks displayed a considerable way above the tops of his gaiters; his hands thrust deep into his breeches pockets; his spectacles high on his bald forehead, and his eyes looking through the open letter that lay before him—through the desk underneath it—through the plank floor, cellars, and foundations of the edifice—and through the entire world into the distant future beyond.

"Four thousand pair of socks," he murmured, pulling down his spectacles and consulting the open letter for the tenth time; "four thousand pair of socks, with the hitch, same as last bale, but a very little coarser in material."

"Four thousand pair! and who's to make them, I

wonder? If poor Mrs. Dorothy Grumbit were here —ah! well, she's gone, so it can't be helped. Four thousand!—dear me, who *will* make them? Do *you* know?"

This question was addressed to his youngest clerk, who sat on the opposite side of the desk staring at Mr. Jollyboy with that open impudence of expression peculiar to young puppy-dogs whose masters are unusually indulgent.

"No, sir, I don't," said the clerk with a broad grin.

Before the perplexed merchant could come at any conclusion on this knotty subject, the door opened, and Martin Rattler entered the room, followed by his friend Barney O'Flannagan.

"You've come to the wrong room, friends," said Mr. Jollyboy with a benignant smile. "My principal clerk engages men and pays wages. His office is just opposite; first door in the passage."

"We don't want to engage," said Martin; "we wish to speak with you, sir."

"Oh, beg pardon!" cried Mr. Jollyboy, leaping off the stool with surprising agility for a man of his years. "Come in this way. Pray be seated. Eh! ah! surely I've seen you before, my good fellow?"

"Yis, sir, that ye have. I've sailed aboard your

ships many a time. My name's Barney O'Flannagan, at yer sarvice."

"Ah! I recollect; and a good man you are, I've been told, Barney. But I have lost sight of you for some years. Been on a long voyage, I suppose?"

"Well, not 'xactly; but I've been on a long cruise, an' no mistake, in the woods o' Brazil. I wos wrecked on the coast there, in the *Firefly*."

"Ah! to be sure. I remember. And your young messmate here, was he with you?"

"Yes, sir, I was," said Martin, answering for himself; "and I had once the pleasure of your acquaintance. Perhaps if you look steadily in my face you may—"

"Ah, then! don't try to bamboozle him. He might as well look at a bit o' mahogany as at your faygur-head. Tell him at wance, Martin, dear."

"Martin?" exclaimed the puzzled old gentleman, seizing the young sailor by the shoulders and gazing intently into his face. "Martin! Martin! Surely not—yes! eh? Martin Rattler?"

"Ay, that am I, dear Mr. Jollyboy, safe and sound, and—"

Martin's speech was cut short in consequence of his being violently throttled by Mr. Jollyboy, who flung his arms round his neck and staggered recklessly about the office with him! This was the great point which Barney had expected—it was the climax to which he had been looking forward all the morning; and it did not come short of his anticipations, for Mr. Jollyboy danced round Martin and embraced him for at least ten minutes, asking him at the same time a shower of questions, which he gave him no time to answer. In the excess of his delight, Barney smote his thigh with his broad hand so forcibly that it burst upon the startled clerk like a pistol-shot, and caused him to spring off his stool!

"Don't be afear'd, young un," said Barney, winking and poking the small clerk jocosely in the ribs with his thumb. "Isn't it beautiful to see them? Arrah, now! isn't it purty?"

"Keep your thumbs to yourself, you sea-monster," said the small clerk angrily, and laying his hand on the ruler. But Barney minded him not, and continued to smite his thigh and rub his hands, while he performed a sort of gigantic war-dance round Mr. Jollyboy and Martin.

In a few minutes the old gentleman subsided sufficiently to understand questions.

"But my aunt," said Martin anxiously; "you have said nothing about Aunt Dorothy. How is she? where is she? is she well?"

To these questions Mr. Jollyboy returned no answer, but sitting suddenly down on a chair, he covered his face with his hands.

"She is not ill?" inquired Martin in a husky voice, while his heart beat violently. "Speak, Mr. Jollyboy, is she—is she—"

"No, she's not ill," returned the old gentleman "but she's—"

"She is dead!" said Martin, in a tone so deep and sorrowful that the old gentleman started up.

"No, no, not dead, my dear boy; I did not mean that. Forgive my stupidity, Martin. Aunt Dorothy is gone—left the village a year ago; and I have never seen or heard of her since."

Terrible though this news was, Martin felt a slight degree of relief to know that she was not dead—at least there was reason to hope that she might be still alive.

"But when did she go? and why? and where?"

"She went about twelve months ago," replied Mr. Jollyboy. "You see, Martin, after she lost you she seemed to lose all hope and all spirit; and at last she gave up making socks for me, and did little but moan in her seat in the window and look out towards the sea. So I got a pleasant young girl to take care of her; and she did not want for any of the comforts of life. One day the little girl came to me here, having run all the way from the village, to say that Mrs. Grumbit had packed up a bundle of clothes and gone off to Liverpool by the coach. She took the opportunity of the girl's absence on some errand to escape, and we should never have known it had not some boys of the village seen her get into the coach and tell the guard that she was going to make inquiries after Martin. I instantly set out for Liverpool; but long before I arrived the coach had discharged its passengers, and the coachman, not suspecting that anything was wrong, had taken no notice of her after arriving. From that day to this I have not ceased to advertise and make all possible inquiries, but without success."

Martin heard the narrative in silence, and when it was finished he sat a few minutes gazing vacantly before him, like one in a dream. Then starting up suddenly, he wrung Mr. Jollyboy's hand. "Good-bye, my dear friend, good-bye. I shall go to Liverpool. We shall meet again."

"Stay, Martin, stay—"

But Martin had rushed from the room, followed by his faithful friend, and in less than half-an-hour they were in the village of Ashford. The coach was to pass in twenty minutes, so bidding Barney engage two outside seats, Martin hastened round by the road towards the cottage. There it stood, quaint, time-worn, and old-fashioned, as when he had last seen it—the little garden in which he had so often played—the bower in which, on fine weather, Aunt Dorothy used to sit, and the door-step on which the white kitten used to gambol. But the shutters were closed and the door was locked, and there was an air of desolation and a deep silence brooding over the place that sank more poignantly into Martin's heart than if he had come and found every vestige of the home of his childhood swept away. It was like the body without the soul. The flowers and stones and well-known forms were there; but she who had given animation to the whole was gone. Sitting down on the door-step, Martin buried his face in his hands and wept.

He was quickly aroused by the bugle of the approaching coach. Springing up, he dashed the tears away and hurried towards the high-road. In a few minutes Barney and he were seated on the top of the coach, and dashing, at the rate of ten miles an hour, along the road to Liverpool.

CHAPTER XXVII.

The old garret.

DAYS and weeks and months passed away, and Martin had searched every nook and corner of the great sea-port without discovering his old aunt, or obtaining the slightest information regarding her. At first he and Barney went about the search together, but after a time he sent his old companion forcibly away to visit his own relatives, who dwelt not far from Bilton, at the same time promising that if he had any good news to tell he would immediately write and let him know.

One morning, as Martin was sitting beside the little fire in his lodging, a tap came to the door, and the servant girl told him that a policeman wished to see him.

"Show him in," said Martin, who was not in the least surprised, for he had had much intercourse with these guardians of the public peace during the course of his unavailing search.

"I think, sir," said the man on entering, "that we've got scent of an old woman w'ich is as like the one that you're arter as hanythink."

Martin rose in haste. "Have you, my man? Are you sure?"

"'Bout as sure as a man can be who never seed her. But it won't take you long to walk. You'd better come and see for yourself."

Without uttering another word, Martin put on his hat and followed the policeman. They passed through several streets and lanes, and at length came to one of the poorest districts of the city, not far distant from the shipping. Turning down a narrow alley, and crossing a low, dirty-looking court, Martin's guide stopped before a door, which he pushed open, and mounted by a flight of rickety wooden stairs to a garret. He opened the door and entered.

"There she is," said the man in a tone of pity, as he pointed to a corner of the apartment; "an' I'm afear'd she's goin' fast."

Martin stepped towards a low truckle-bed on which lay the emaciated form of a woman covered with a scanty and ragged quilt. The corner of it was drawn across her face, and so gentle was her breathing that it seemed as if she were already dead. Martin removed the covering, and one glance at that gentle, careworn countenance sufficed to convince him that his old aunt lay before him. His first impulse was to seize her in his strong arms, but another look at the frail and attenuated form caused him to shrink back in fear.

"Leave me," he said, rising hastily and slipping half a sovereign into the policeman's hand; "this is she. I wish to be alone with her."

The man touched his hat and retired, closing the door behind him; while Martin, sitting down on the bed, took one of his aunt's thin hands in his. The action was tenderly performed, but it awoke her. For the first time it flashed across Martin's mind that the sudden joy of seeing him might be too much for one so feeble as Aunt Dorothy seemed to be. He turned his back hastily to the light, and with a violent effort suppressed his feelings while he asked how she did.

"Well, very well," said Aunt Dorothy, in a faint voice. "Are you the missionary that was here long ago? Oh! I've been longing for you. Why did you not come to read to me oftener about Jesus? But I have had him here although you did not come. He has been saying, 'Come unto me, ye that labour and are heavy laden, and I will give you rest.' Yes, I have found rest in him." She ceased and seemed to fall asleep again; but in a few seconds she opened her eyes and said, "Martin, too, has been to see me; but he does not come so often now. The darling boy used always to come to me in my dreams. But he never brings me food. Why does no one ever bring me food? I am hungry."

"Should you like food now, if I brought it to you?" said Martin in a low voice.

"Yes, yes, bring me food; I am dying."

Martin released her hand and glided gently out of the room. In a few minutes he returned with a can of warm soup and a roll, of which Aunt Dorothy partook with an avidity that showed she had been in urgent need. Immediately after she went to sleep, and Martin sat upon the bed holding her hand in both of his till she awoke, which she did in an hour after, and again ate a little food. While she was thus engaged the door opened and a young man entered, who stated that he was a doctor, and had been sent there by a policeman.

"There is no hope," he said in a whisper, after feeling her pulse; "the system is quite exhausted."

"Doctor," whispered Martin, seizing the young man by the arm, "can nothing save her? I have money, and can command *anything* that may do her good."

The doctor shook his head. "You may give her a

little wine. It will strengthen her for a time, but I fear there is no hope. I will send in a bottle if you wish it."

Martin gave him the requisite sum, and in a few minutes the wine was brought up by a boy.

The effect of the wine was wonderful. Aunt Dorothy's eyes sparkled as they used to do in days of old, and she spoke with unwonted energy.

"You are kind to me, young man," she said, looking earnestly into Martin's face, which, however, he kept carefully in shadow. "May our Lord reward you!"

"Would you like me to talk to you of your nephew?" said Martin. "I have seen him abroad."

"Seen my boy! Is he not dead?"

"No; he is alive, and in this country, too."

Aunt Dorothy turned pale, but did not reply for a few minutes, during which she grasped his hand convulsively.

"Turn your face to the light," she said faintly.

Martin obeyed, and bending over her whispered, "He is here; I am Martin, my dear, dear aunt—"

No expression of surprise escaped from Aunt Dorothy as she folded her arms round his neck and pressed his head upon her bosom. His hot tears fell upon her neck while she held him, but she spoke not.

It was evident that as the strength infused by the wine abated her faculties became confused. At length she whispered,—

"It is good of you to come to see me, darling boy. You have often come to me in my dreams. But do not leave me so soon; stay a very little longer."

"This is no dream, dearest aunt," whispered Martin, while his tears flowed faster; "I am really here."

"Ay, so you always say, my darling child; but you always go away and leave me. This is a dream, no doubt, like all the rest; but oh, it seems very, very real! You never *wept* before, although you often smiled. Surely this is the best and brightest dream I ever had!"

Continuing to murmur his name while she clasped him tightly to her bosom, Aunt Dorothy gently fell asleep.

CHAPTER XXVIII.

Conclusion.

AUNT DOROTHY GRUMBIT did *not* die. Her gentle spirit had nearly fled; but Martin's return and Martin's tender nursing brought her round, and she gradually regained all her former strength and vigour. Yes, to the unutterable joy of Martin, to the inexpressible delight of Mr. Arthur Jollyboy and Barney, and to the surprise and complete discomfiture of the young doctor, who shook his head and said, " There is no hope," Aunt Dorothy Grumbit recovered, and was brought back in health and in triumph to her old cottage at Ashford!

Moreover, she was arrayed again in the old bed-curtain chintz with the flowers as big as saucers, and the old high-crowned cap. A white kitten was got, too, so like the one that used to be Martin's playmate, that no one could discover a hair of difference. So remarkable was this, that Martin made inquiry, and found that it was actually the grand-daughter of the old kitten, which was still alive and well; so he brought it back too, and formally installed it in the cottage along with its grandchild.

There was a great house-warming on the night of the day in which Aunt Dorothy Grumbit was brought back. Mr. Arthur Jollyboy was there—of course; and the vicar was there; and the pursy doctor who used to call Martin "a scamp;" and the schoolmaster; and last, though not least, Barney O'Flannagan was there. And they all had tea, during which dear Aunt Dorothy smiled sweetly on everybody and said nothing—and, indeed, did nothing, except that once or twice she put additional sugar and cream into Martin's cup when he was not looking, and stroked one of his hands continually. After tea Martin related his adventures in Brazil, and Barney helped him; and these two talked more that night than any one could have believed it possible for human beings to do, without the aid of steam lungs! And the doctor listened, and the vicar and schoolmaster questioned, and old Mr. Jollyboy roared and laughed till he became purple in the face—particularly at the sallies of Barney. As for old Aunt Dorothy Grumbit, she listened when Martin spoke. When Martin was silent she became stone deaf!

In the course of time Mr. Jollyboy made Martin his head clerk; and then, becoming impatient, he made him his partner off-hand. Then he made Barney O'Flannagan an overseer in the warehouses; and when the duties of the day were over, the versatile Irishman became his confidential servant, and went to sup and sleep at the Old Hulk; which, he used to remark, was quite a natural and proper and decidedly comfortable place to come to an anchor in.

Martin became the stay and comfort of his aunt in her old age, and the joy which he was the means of giving to her heart was like a deep and placid river which never ceases to flow. Ah! there is a rich blessing in store for those who tenderly nurse and comfort the aged, when called upon to do so; and assuredly there is a sharp thorn prepared for those who neglect this sacred duty. Martin read the Bible to her night and morning; and she did nothing but watch for him at the window while he was out. As Martin afterwards became an active member of the benevolent societies with which his partner was connected, he learned from sweet experience that " it is more blessed to give than to receive," and that " it is *better* to go to the house of mourning than to go to the house of feasting."

Dear young reader, do not imagine that we plead in favour of moroseness or gloom. Laugh if you will, and feast if you will, and remember, too, that "a merry heart is a continual feast;" but we pray you not to forget that God himself has said that a visit to the house of mourning is *better* than a visit to the house of feasting. And strange to say, it is productive of greater joy; for to do good is better than to get good, as surely as sympathy is better than selfishness.

Martin visited the poor and read the Bible to them; and in watering others he was himself watered, for he found the "Pearl of Great Price," even Jesus Christ, the Saviour of the world.

Business prospered in the hands of Martin Rattler, too, and he became a man of substance. Naturally, too, he became a man of great importance in the town of Bilton. The quantity of work that Martin and Mr. Jollyboy and Barney used to get through was quite marvellous, and the number of engagements they had during the course of a day was quite bewildering.

In the existence of all men, who are not born to unmitigated misery, there are times and seasons of peculiar enjoyment. The happiest hour of all the twenty-four to Martin Rattler was the hour of seven in the evening; for then it was that he found himself seated before the blazing fire in the parlour of the Old Hulk, to which Aunt Dorothy Grumbit had consented to be removed, and in which she was now a fixture. Then it was that old Mr. Jollyboy beamed with benevolence, until the old lady sometimes thought the fire was going to melt him; then it was that the tea-kettle sang on the hob like a canary; and then it was that Barney bustled about the room preparing the evening meal, and talking all the time with the most perfect freedom to any one who chose to listen to him. Yes, seven p.m. was Martin's great hour, and Aunt Dorothy's great hour, and old Mr. Jollyboy's great hour, and Barney's too; for each knew that the labours of the day were done, and that the front door was locked for the night, and that a great talk was brewing.

They had a tremendous talk every night, sometimes on one subject, sometimes on another; but the subject of all others that they talked oftenest about was their travels. And many a time and oft, when the winter storms howled round the Old Hulk, Barney was invited to draw in his chair, and Martin and he plunged again vigorously into the great old forests of South America, and spoke so feelingly about them that Aunt Dorothy and Mr.

Jollyboy almost fancied themselves transported into the midst of tropical scenes, and felt as if they were surrounded by parrots, and monkeys, and jaguars, and alligators, and anacondas, and all the wonderful birds, beasts, reptiles, and fishes that inhabit the woods and waters of Brazil.

THE END.

Lightning Source UK Ltd.
Milton Keynes UK
UKHW020419050522
402512UK00003B/158